# BritishDesign
# 2007/08

Branding and Graphic Design
Packaging Design
New Media Design
Interior, Retail and Event Design
Product Design

**BIS PUBLISHERS**
Herengracht 370-372
1016 CH Amsterdam
P.O Box 323
1000 AH Amsterdam
The Netherlands
T +31 (0)20 524 7560
F +31 (0)20 524 7557
bis@bispublishers.nl
www.bispublishers.nl

© 2007 BIS Publishers, Amsterdam

ISBN 978-90-6369-137-0

B/S

# BritishDesign
## 2007/08

Branding and Graphic Design
Packaging Design
New Media Design
Interior, Retail and Event Design
Product Design

# Contents

008 **Foreword**
by Rudolf van Wezel

010 **Innovation, Style and Wit...**
**British Design 2007/08**
by Adrian Shaughnessy

**Branding and Graphic Design**
018 35 Communications
020 Alembic Design Consultants
022 biz-R
024 Budding
026 Buzzword Creative
028 The Cake Group
030 Checkland Kindleysides Ltd
032 Clusta Ltd
034 Enigma Creative Solutions Ltd
036 Enterprise IG
038 Felton Communication
040 Fitch
042 Fluid
046 The Formation Creative Consultants Ltd
048 Hemisphere
050 Kemistry
054 Kino Design
056 La Boca
058 Linney Design
062 Lisa Tse Ltd
066 Lloyd Northover
068 NE6 Design Consultants
070 Parent
072 pi global
074 +Prism.Brand.Architects
076 Rareform London
078 Redpath
080 Reinvigorate
082 SCG London
084 Springetts
086 Start Creative Ltd
090 Studio Output
092 Tango Design
094 TWO:design
096 Über
098 Un.titled
100 Z3

**Packaging Design**
104 Blackburn's Ltd
106 dare!
108 Enterprise IG
110 Identica
112 jones knowles ritchie
114 Osborne Pike
116 pi global
118 Pure Equator
122 Reach
124 Springetts
126 Stocks Taylor Benson Ltd
128 Two by Two
130 Vibrandt
132 Ziggurat Brands

**New Media Design**
136 Clusta Ltd
138 ClustaSpace
140 Creative Edge
142 Enterprise IG
144 Lloyd Northover
146 Pod1
148 Start Creative Ltd
152 unit9.
154 UsTwo
156 View

**Interior, Retail and Event Design**
160 BDP Design
162 Briggs Hillier Design
164 CampbellRigg
168 Checkland Kindleysides Ltd
170 Corsie Naysmith Design
172 Dalziel and Pow
174 Enigma Creative Solutions Ltd
176 Enterprise IG
178 Fitch
180 JHP Design
182 Kinnersley Kent design
184 Land Design Studio Ltd
186 Reinvigorate
188 Sheridan & Co
190 Start Creative Ltd
192 Tibbatts Associates Ltd
194 Two by Two
196 Philip Watts Design

**Product Design**
200 3form Design
202 fearsomengine
204 FSW Design Limited
206 Jab Design
208 Kinneir Dufort
210 Andrew Lang Product Design Limited
212 Maddison Limited
214 Tangerine Product Design
216 TKO Design

218 **Advertisements**

228 **Call for Entries**

230 **Participating Agencies by Location**

234 **Addresses**

240 **Publication Data**

# Design Agencies by Location

**01 Andover**
3form Design

**02 Bath**
Osborne Pike

**03 Birmingham**
Clusta Ltd
ClustaSpace
Fluid
+Prism.Brand.Architects
Tibbatts Associates Ltd
Z3

**04 Bournemouth**
Parent

**05 Bristol**
Kinneir Dufort
Reach

**06 Chichester**
Buzzword Creative

**07 Coventry**
Budding

**08 Edinburgh**
Redpath

**09 Enderby**
Stocks Taylor Benson Ltd

**10 Eton**
Enigma Creative Solutions Ltd

**11 Fittleworth**
Maddison Limited

**12 Glasgow**
fearsomengine

**13 Halifax**
Reinvigorate

**14 Hitchin**
Alembic Design Consultants

**15 Kew**
Land Design Studio Ltd

**16 Leeds**
dare!

**17 Leicester**
Checkland Kindleysides Ltd
Sheridan & Co
Un.titled

**18 Liverpool**
Jab Design

**19 London**
35 Communications
BDP Design
Blackburn's Ltd
The Cake Group
CampbellRigg
Corsie Naysmith Design
Dalziel and Pow
Enterprise IG
Felton Communication
Fitch
The Formation Creative Consultants Ltd
Indentica
JHP Design
jones knowles ritchie
Kemistry
Kinnersley Kent design
Kino Design
La Boca
Andrew Lang Product Design Limited
Lisa Tse Ltd
Lloyd Northover
pi global
Pod1
Rareform London
SCG London
Sheridan & Co
Springetts
Start Creative Ltd
Tangerine Product Design
Tango Design
TKO Design
Two by Two
TWO:design
Unit9.
UsTwo
View
Ziggurat Brands

**20 Lutterworth**
Briggs Hillier Design

**21 Manchester**
Hemisphere

**22 Mansfield**
Linney Design

**23 Newcastle upon Tyne**
NE6 Design Consultants

**24 Nottingham**
FSW Design Limited
Pure Equator
Studio Output
Philip Watts Design

**25 Sheffield**
Über

**26 Totnes**
biz-R

**27 Truro**
Creative Edge

**28 Windsor**
Vibrandt

# Foreword

Welcome to *British Design 2007/08*, the third edition of BIS Publishers' cross-section of design studios and creative consultancies in Britain. We are proud to offer the British creative industry and its domestic and international clients this completely new, third survey of creative talent from the UK. The changes in the design industry over the last two years are of course reflected in this book: a lot of new names now present themselves for the first time, along with many established firms that are in here again because they have experienced the benefits of getting their work out to the national and international audience of design buyers who use the book.

The goal of this book is simple: to help clients in their search for the ideal design partner. *British Design 2007/08* provides an instant impression of each participating agency's work – it is a reference tool for whenever professional creative input is needed.

In his introductory article Adrian Shaughnessy notes that globalisation, which has the tendency to create sameness, not difference, is an obstacle for the British design scene to overcome. Because it is difference that creates interest and engagement. With its marriage of the creative and the pragmatic, British design has all that it takes to stay ahead of the game. To do so, it needs its clients to recognise not only the economical and strategic benefits of good design, but also the magic that good design can produce – that intangible but very important element that makes good design good for the soul, as one of Shaughnessy's clients once said.

Keep that in mind when you talk with one of the fine agencies in this book.

Rudolf van Wezel
BIS Publishers

# Innovation, Style and Wit...
# British Design 2007/08

by Adrian Shaughnessy

I once had a client. He was a tough-minded businessman who ran a successful group of companies. Through the bold introduction of advanced technology, he had transformed his business from a slumbering loss-making entity into a dynamic and profitable mini-empire. To reflect the changes that he had made, he appointed my studio to revamp the group's brand identity.

At the end of the lengthy design process – a procedure that involved the creation of a family of logos, a range of corporate literature, templates for press adverts, signage and a suite of websites – he called me to say that he was pleased with the outcome. He explained that he'd had a good response to the new identity from both his customers and his staff, and he mentioned that he was pleased with the strategic benefits the new 'look' had brought him. He called it 'a successful repositioning'. Like most clients he had a good-natured moan about the cost, but then he added an unexpected afterthought: 'I can see that good design is good for the soul,' he said.

He was a nuts-and-bolts, value-for-money guy, and throughout the creative process he'd given no indication that he saw graphic design as anything other than a purely mechanistic process. And yet, here he was, admitting that design had a benefit beyond the purely strategic. I was surprised, but also pleased.

This 'feel-good' factor which we often find in design is hard to quantify. We know it exists, but it's intangible. It's much easier to discuss the economic and strategic benefits of good design, since these are benefits that can be measured. And as a consequence, the strategic use of design is now central to business planning. Today, there are no industries that can afford to ignore design: printed and digital communications must be sophisticated and attractive items; consumers will no longer buy shoddy goods – product design is the key to creating desirable products; shoppers will not be enticed into dull shops and poorly designed environments – retail design is requited to make shopping into an entertaining activity. But we shouldn't forget that design makes the world a better place. As my client said – it's good for the soul.

## The New Wonder Ingredient

In his book *Tom Peters Essentials: Design*, the influential management guru has become a surprising advocate of the power of design. He puts forward the case that design is the main factor in determining whether a product or service will stand out. The American writer Virgina Postrel, in her book *The Substance of Style*, goes further. She has noted that we have entered the age of aesthetics: '...the look and feel of people, places, and things is increasingly important as a source of value, both economic and cultural.' Postrel goes on to say: 'Aesthetics shows up where function used to be the only thing that mattered, from toilet brushes to business memos to computers and cell phones. And people's expectations keep rising... If you're in business, you have to invest in aesthetics simply to keep up with the competition.'

The value of good design – the marriage of function and aesthetics – is something that we've always known about in Great Britain. Traditionally, only the rich could afford to surround themselves with well-designed products. But with the onset of mass prosperity (from the 1960s onwards) design was no longer the exclusive preserve of the affluent. Nowadays, good design is found everywhere, and this has resulted in the transformation of everyday life.

London is arguably the style capital of the world. Tourists still flock to the city to see The Tower of London and Buckingham Palace, but many thousands also come to see, and buy, London style. They come to visit shops, museums, galleries, music venues, and they come to absorb the countless manifestations of UK design – products, fashion, graphics and environments.

## Official Recognition

Even the British government has woken up to the importance of design. The Department for Culture Media and Sport is responsible for the UK's 'Creative Industries', a sector it defines as 'those industries that are based on individual creativity, skill and talent. They are also those that have the potential to create wealth and jobs through developing intellectual property.' A report published by the UK's Department of Trade and Industry on its website (www.dti.gov.uk/files/file21906.pdf) notes that '...UK creative industries contributed 8.9% to GDP, compared with circa 3% from manufacturing…total creative industry exports contributed £11.6 billion in 2003 (DCMS, 2005).'

Of course, when management gurus and government departments talk about design, they are talking about design in the widest sense of the term. Graphic design is only a part of that glittering array. But it's a hugely important part. Patrick Burgoyne, editor of *Creative Review*, the leading journal of creativity in design and advertising, is a seasoned observer of the international graphic design scene: 'Graphic design is one of the few industries in which Britain still punches above its weight as a nation,' he notes, 'and it looks set to continue that way. We have our eminent elder statesmen and women, but also a new wave of independent studios ready to carry on the spirit of innovation, style and wit, allied to superb craftsmanship, which has become the hallmark of the UK graphics scene."

## Everybody Needs Good Design

Graphic design creates the metaphorical packaging that enables so much of the British creative sector to flourish. It's at the heart of nearly all creative activities. Fashion houses need graphic designers to create ads and websites; architects use graphic designers to produce signage and other types of communication; the music industry – despite the rise of digital downloading – still commissions vast amounts of innovative graphic design; so too do the film and television industries, computer gaming and advertising. Without typographers, illustrators, retouchers, web designers and art directors, the postwar British design revolution might never have happened.

The best British graphic design mixes high-end creativity with precise communication. The business community demands that design is focused on the end user with deadly accuracy. Sometimes, it has to be admitted, this can lead to the creation of blandness: so much effort goes into research, focus groups and consumer targeting that creativity is forgotten, or at best, ironed out of the equation. Yet, when designers – working closely with their clients – get the balance right between customer focus and intuitive creativity, the results are often remarkable.

## The Digital Realm

British designers were quick to enter the digital realm, and today, in a world of media convergence, graphic designers are effortlessly moving between web design, moving image installations and mobile communications. A new generation of computer-savvy consumers now uses the Internet to shop and to check for price comparisons. Websites must be easy to use and packed with information, but they must also be stylish.

Digital communications are already profoundly changing the way we live. Our mobile phones, to take just one example, have become data points; the tiny screens already supply us with animation, images, text and sound. We can use our phones to book tickets, pay for municipal services and interact with all sorts of institutions. The mobile phone is no longer just a phone: it is a camera, a music player, and increasingly, a communications hub.

The digital realm has migrated into the bricks and mortar world of shopping; touch screens are everywhere. Nokia has recently launched a chain of luxurious flagship stores in the world's great capitals that offer the sort of screen based audio-visual experience – created mainly by British on-screen specialists – that is normally only found in night clubs, museums and art galleries. Soon, the breakfast table will be invaded by digital communications. A pundit writing in the British magazine *Design Week* (the world's only weekly design journal) notes that: '…what is currently a rather passive piece of packaging for cornflakes will converge with other forms of media so that the cereal pack will play a short animation for the kids and a recipe or audio track for mum…' Shopping will never be the same. There is no limit to digital proliferation and the opportunities it offers to clients and smart designers. But technological advances offering new platforms of communication are worthless unless they are brought alive by smart ideas and creative execution.

## The Physical Realm

Britain has always created iconic products. The red London bus, the Mini, the Dyson vacuum cleaner, the Kenwood Chef, the Polyprop chair and the cordless kettle are quintessentially British, and show how Brit designers excel at creating memorable artifacts that combine design and practicality with a touch of eccentricity. In 2005, a prime time TV series, Made for the Masses, was devoted to this strand of British design history. As the programme's director said: 'I see the series as an attempt to show how good design doesn't have to be expensive or exclusive – to claw back design from the designer label. If you find something valuable and useful in your life then that is what good design is. Made for the Masses will reawaken interest in everyday designs that fulfill practical and emotional as well as aesthetic needs.' But good products need to be sold in congenial and inviting environments. Accordingly, retail design is now one of the most sophisticated and complex areas of design innovation. The best retail environments are places of entertainment, as well as locations to buy 'stuff'; and window design – think Selfridges, Harvey Nichols – provides visual entertainment to rival art galleries and museums. Shopping has become a sensory experience.

**The View from Abroad**

Living and working in Britain, we see this stuff regularly, and we see new design emerging daily. But how does an international audience view British design? Judging by the number of overseas clients making use of UK design expertise, we are bound to conclude that Brit design is highly regarded around the world. All the big design consultancies work abroad and many giant corporations choose to buy British design skills at a time when, thanks to globalization, they are free to purchase design from anywhere they chose.

For an objective view, I asked the American design writer Steven Heller what he thought about British design. Heller has written over 80 books on design and is regularly commissioned by the design press to comment on trends and developments in global design. Heller says this: 'Just as I always looked to the UK for the most progressive pop music (I'm still a Beatles fanatic), films and art, I still look to the UK for graphic design innovations. I'm not sure why this is. But maybe because in this globalized world I wish there were still visual language differences. The UK is, at a glance, closest to the US, and yet it is a parallel world. Britain has a design culture that demands adherence.'

Heller's view is typical of many observers of the British scene. But if Brit design is to remain at the forefront of modern visual communications it has to overcome an array of obstacles, and the most formidable of these is globalisation. As Steven Heller notes above, globalisation has a tendency to create sameness, not difference – and it is difference that creates interest and engagement. But it's not hard to imagine that British design, with its marriage of the creative and the pragmatic, with its long history of excellence, has the intellectual, business and creative dexterity to stay ahead of the game.

It's just a guess, but ten years from now, the 2017 version of this book will still contain some of the best design the world has to offer. You might be reading it on your mobile phone, or some other futuristic medium, but it will remain an essential document for anyone who wants to keep up with the sharp end of visual invention.

# 35 Communications
## The Corporate Branding and Reporting Specialists

Clearwater Yard / 35 Inverness Street /
London NW1 7HB
T +44 (0)20 7428 9960
hello@35communications.com
www.35communications.com

**Management** Keith Bamber, Nigel Forsyth, Lee Hoddy, Thom Newton **Contact** Lindie Champion **Staff** 22 **Founded** 2003 **Memberships** CIM, CID, CIMA, Prince's Trust Mentors

### Company Profile
We are a branding and design agency who understands the commercial benefits that good brands should bring. Our strength lies in creating, evolving and repositioning an organisation's brand to help them perform better, whatever the demands of the industry or environment.

### Philosophy
We use design not only to create and deliver brands, but also to raise issues, facilitate debate and find solutions. So when clients work with us, we expect them to take part in the process, review their values, evaluate their communications and take ownership of their brand.

### Core Disciplines
We work on all aspects of branding – naming, brand creation, repositioning, implementation and ongoing support and management, in both print and online.

### Milestones
– We're the team behind the new 101 brand, the Single Non Emergency Number. It's the biggest communications initiative ever undertaken by The Home Office.
– We developed a new brand identity & positioning for the Royal Albert Hall – 'The Nation's Hall, The World's Stage'.
– We helped The Learning & Skills Council save a projected £2m through a new literature & communications system.

### Some of Our Clients Include
COI, Diageo, Dyslexia Action, The Health Foundation, The Home Office, National Express Group, Northern Foods, Reed Elsevier, Royal Albert Hall and Wolseley.

1  Annual Review, Diageo, 2005/6
2  101 Brand Identity, Home Office, 2006
3  Brand Identity, Science Learning Centres, 2004/5
4  Brand Identity, UK Biobank, 2005

A NEW NUMBER TO CALL ☎ **101** WHEN IT'S LESS URGENT THAN **999**

GEO

Science
LEARNING CENTRES

**biobank** uk
Improving the health of future generations

# Alembic Design Consultants
## Communications Design

Bancroft House / 34 Bancroft / Hitchin SG5 1LA
T +44 (0)1462 435 441
info@alembic.co.uk
www.alembic.co.uk

**Contact** Jonathan Miller
**Founded** 1995

### Company Profile
Alembic is an independent design consultancy
focused on clear and effective communications.

We work on long-term strategic projects and smaller
scale one-off communications with clients of all kinds,
from small charities to large public companies in
London, the UK, Europe and elsewhere.

Equally committed to creativity and client needs,
the Alembic approach is based on careful distillation
of essential information, attention to substance
and structure; and awareness of context, schedule
and budget.

Typical projects include corporate literature and
annual reports, marketing communications and
websites. We create new corporate and consumer
brands, and devise strategies to develop and manage
existing brand identities.

### Clients
Asset Value Investors
Ceema Technology
CS Healthcare
Datamonitor
Eurosport
Fletcher Priest Architects
First Islamic Investment Bank
Granada Media
Merrill Lynch Europe
Petrogal
Portugal Telecom
Regents Business School London
Sport England
The Film Editors
Villeroy & Boch

1 Tower 42 wayfinding system, Fletcher Priest
  Architects
2 Website and brand identity, Hamilton
3 Prospectus and brand redeployment,
  Regents Business School London
4 Annual report, Sport England
5 Brand identity, The Film Editors
6 Brand identity, Asset Value Investors

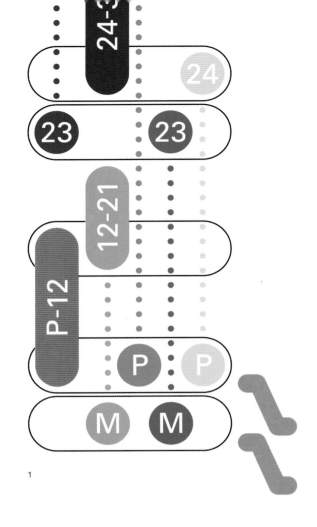

3

2

1

4

5

AVI

6

2

# biz-R

35a Fore Street / Totnes / Devon TQ9 5HN
T +44 (0)1803 868 989 / F +44 (0)1803 868 888
look@biz-r.co.uk
www.biz-r.co.uk

**Management** Blair Thomson
**Contacts** Blair Thomson, Tish England
**Staff** 5 **Founded** 1996

## Company Profile
Founded in 1996 biz-R has established a reputation for its progressive execution in graphic design. While our size and working philosophy are consistent with a small specialist creative practice, our talents are as varied as those found within large graphic design firms, enabling us to provide an equally diverse range of clients with the best of both worlds: personal attention and design innovation. This unique combination underlies our ability to produce outstanding design solutions and valuable long-term client relationships.

We are a full-service design studio. Our capabilities extend across print and digital media. We have expertise in the creation of identity systems, branding, print communications, packaging and interactive design & development. Our focus is to implement forward thinking solutions for every form of communication.

## Company Motivation
_ Ideas
_ Passion
_ Style with substance
_ Creativity
_ Relationships
_ Culture
_ Reliability

## Company Objectives
_ Attract attention
_ Alter attitudes
_ Change perspectives
_ Heighten perceptions
_ Create interest
_ Challenge all mediums
_ Prompt responses
_ Deliver results

Objective /

Enga

Process /

Listen / Explore / Challenge / Inspire / Develop / Innovate / Diversify / Communicate / Engage / Respond / Deliver /

Examples /

# ge

**Verb /**
To occupy, attract, or involve (someone's interest
or attention)

**Adjective /**
(Designer, or their works) morally committed to
a particular aim or cause

# Budding
## Graphic Design

67 Poplar Road / Earlsdon / Coventry CV5 6FX
T +44 (0)24 7671 4805
info@buddingdesign.com
www.buddingdesign.com

**Contact** Katy Miranda
**Founded** 2000

We supply graphic design in the form of brand design, design for print, and websites.

Working with businesses to overhaul their current image or working with entrepreneurs to define a new company, we aim to provide specific no-nonsense design that can be understood visually by the potential client, as well as lived with by the company.

1 SMP Plastics – Rebrand
2 Leos Group – New Business
3 Net of Light – New Business
4 Bond & Associates – Rebrand
5 Fifty–fifty Language Services – Rebrand
6 Acutec – Rebrand
7 Kamala Blue – New Business
8 Lowries Art – Rebrand

1

2

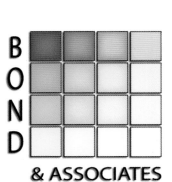

3

4

Brand, Graphic
& Website Design

5

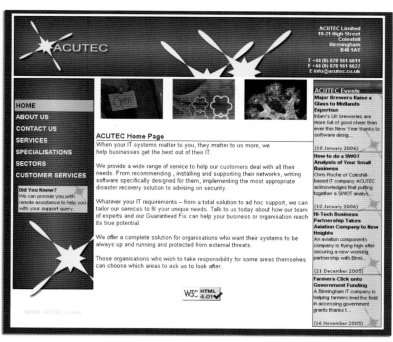

ACUTEC Limited
19-21 High Street
Coleshill
Birmingham
B46 1AY

T +44 (0) 870 161 6611
F +44 (0) 870 161 6622
E info@acutec.co.uk

HOME
ABOUT US
CONTACT US
SERVICES
SPECIALISATIONS
SECTORS
CUSTOMER SERVICES

**Did You Know?**
We can provide you with remote assistance to help you with your support query.

**ACUTEC Home Page**

When your IT systems matter to you, they matter to us more, we help businesses get the best out of their IT.

We provide a wide range of service to help our customers deal with all their needs. From recommending , installing and supporting their networks, writing software specifically designed for them, implementing the most appropriate disaster recovery solution to advising on security.

Whatever your IT requirements -- from a total solution to ad hoc support, we can tailor our services to fit your unique needs. Talk to us today about how our team of experts and our Guaranteed Fix can help your business or organisation reach its true potential.

We offer a complete solution for organisations who want their systems to be always up and running and protected from external threats.

Those organisations who wish to take responsibility for some areas themselves can choose which areas to ask us to look after.

©2006 - ACUTEC Limited

**ACUTEC Events**

**Major Brewers Raise a Glass to Midlands Expertise**
Inbev's UK breweries are more full of good cheer than ever this New Year thanks to software desig...
(18 January 2006)

**How to do a SWOT Analysis of Your Small Business**
Chris Roche of Coleshill-based IT company ACUTEC acknowledges that putting together a SWOT analys...
(10 January 2006)

**Hi-Tech Business Partnership Takes Aviation Company to New Heights**
An aviation components company is flying high after securing a new working partnership with Birmi...
(21 December 2005)

**Farmers Click onto Government Funding**
A Birmingham IT company is helping farmers lead the field in accessing government grants thanks t...
(16 November 2005)

6

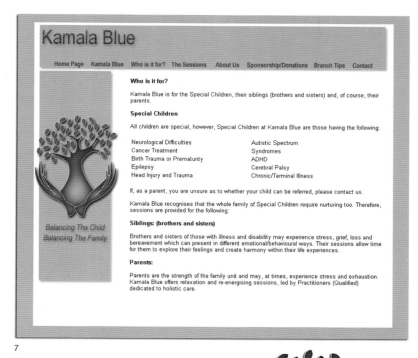

Kamala Blue

Home Page    Kamala Blue    Who is it for?    The Sessions    About Us    Sponsorship/Donations    Branch Tips    Contact

**Who is it for?**

Kamala Blue is for the Special Children, their siblings (brothers and sisters) and, of course, their parents.

**Special Children**

All children are special, however, Special Children at Kamala Blue are those having the following:

| | |
|---|---|
| Neurological Difficulties | Autistic Spectrum |
| Cancer Treatment | Syndromes |
| Birth Trauma or Prematurity | ADHD |
| Epilepsy | Cerebral Palsy |
| Head Injury and Trauma | Chronic/Terminal Illness |

If, as a parent, you are unsure as to whether your child can be referred, please contact us.

Kamala Blue recognises that the whole family of Special Children require nurturing too. Therefore, sessions are provided for the following:

**Siblings: (brothers and sisters)**

Brothers and sisters of those with illness and disability may experience stress, grief, loss and bereavement which can present in different emotional/behavioural ways. Their sessions allow time for them to explore their feelings and create harmony within their life experiences.

**Parents:**

Parents are the strength of the family unit and may, at times, experience stress and exhaustion. Kamala Blue offers relaxation and re-energising sessions, led by Practitioners (Qualified) dedicated to holistic care.

*Balancing The Child*
*Balancing The Family*

7

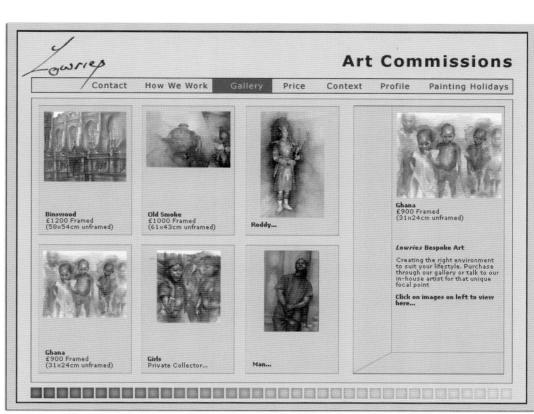

**Art Commissions**

Contact    How We Work    Gallery    Price    Context    Profile    Painting Holidays

**Binswood**
£1200 Framed
(58x54cm unframed)

**Old Smoke**
£1000 Framed
(61x43cm unframed)

**Roddy...**

**Ghana**
£900 Framed
(31x24cm unframed)

*Lowries* Bespoke Art

Creating the right environment to suit your lifestyle. Purchase through our gallery or talk to our in-house artist for that unique focal point.

**Click on images on left to view here...**

**Ghana**
£900 Framed
(31x24cm unframed)

**Girls**
Private Collector...

**Man...**

8

# Buzzword Creative

146 St Pancras / Chichester PO19 7SH /
West Sussex
T +44 (0)1243 792 146 / F +44 (0)1243 787 272
adam@buzzwordcreative.co.uk
www.buzzwordcreative.co.uk

**Contact** Adam Smith
**Staff** 8

**Company Profile**
We have always believed that a balance of fresh
thinking and intelligent design is key to communicating
brand strength and promoting business success.
By combining original ideas with a clear objective-
focused approach, we never lose sight of our clients'
business needs.

**Clients include**
AGI Media
APACS – the UK payments association
Barclays
BBC
Bristows
Chip and PIN
Dental Protection
EDS
Home Office
PEI Genesis
NatWest
Royal Armouries
Royal Bank of Scotland
Royal Naval Benevolent Trust
Vodafone
West Sussex County Council
Wiley

1  Chip and PIN identifier
2  www.hoppersworkshop.co.uk
3  Wiley scientific and technical book jackets
4  Home Office 'Identity Theft' campaign
5  BBC 'Rapido' promotional DVD packaging
6  EDS 48-sheet billboard campaign

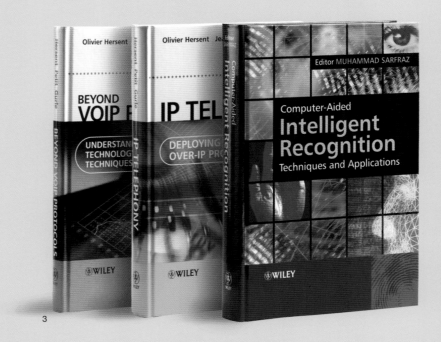

4

5

**Commitment**

At EDS customer satisfaction is top of our agenda. That's why we constantly strive to provide
our clients with effective, innovative solutions to all their IT problems, whatever they may be.
For more information visit www.eds.com

EDS

6

# The Cake Group

10 Stephen Mews / London W1T 1AG
T +44 (0)20 7307 3100 / F +44 (0)20 7307 3101
andrea@cakegroup.com
www.cakegroup.com

**Management** Mike Mathieson, Mark Whelan,
Adrian Pettett **Contact** Andrea Ledsham
**Staff** 60 **Founded** 1999

Cake is the market leader in brand entertainment.
The agency, which has been pioneering brand
entertainment for 6 years, employs a varied and
talented workforce of 60 people.

Cake's approach for clients is to find the most
effective communication route in which to engage
the consumer, then match that with exceptional
creativity. Events, PR, digital, ad-funded programmes
or design – Cake is on a mission to entertain
audiences.

Brand entertainment is at the heart of the Cake
proposition and has remained there as the company
has grown from the staff of 8 in 1999 to today's 60
staff members operating out of their HQ over 3 floors
in Fitzrovia, central London.

Client list includes leading companies such
as Orange, Unilever, Reebok, Coors, COI
communications, Motorola, Nintendo and Bacardi.

**OF LIFE TO MUSIC**

BERTOLLI

BEST EVER TASTE

FREE BREWOMETER™

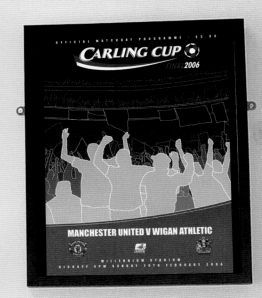

OFFICIAL MATCHDAY PROGRAMME · £5.00

CARLING CUP FINAL 2006

MANCHESTER UNITED V WIGAN ATHLETIC

MILLENNIUM STADIUM
KICKOFF 3PM SUNDAY 26TH FEBRUARY 2006

HILL STREET BLUES

**cake**
BRAND ENTERTAINMENT

BEN & JERRY'S

**Sundae**
ON THE COMMON

29th - 30th July 2006
Clapham Common
12 noon til 8pm

**Saturday 29th**
Badly Drawn Boy
ECHO & THE BUNNYMEN

**Sunday 30th**
José González
The Wonder Stuff

CAPTAIN

Roland Shanks
Tiny Dancers

LISA LINDLEY - JONES

It's pure summer fun

Admission £5

Ticket sales

**Refreshing London**

Lipton Ice Tea

last chance
to work from
the first ever
outdoor office

**hoxton sq
9–11 august**

book free
online now

DRINK BETTER*

free fully functional outdoor office space including
receptionist, waiting area, bookable meeting rooms,
wi-fi hot desks, free refreshments and more

book free online now
www.liptonicetea.co.uk

# Checkland Kindleysides Ltd

Charnwood Edge / Cossington / Leicester LE7 4UZ /
Leicestershire
T +44 (0)116 2644 700 / F +44 (0)116 2644 701
info@checkind.com
www.checkind.com

**Management** Jeff Kindleysides; Claire Callaway,
Managing Director
**Staff** 85 **Founded** 1979

## Company Profile
We are an independent design group and we believe
our culture is unique. We're collaborative, inventive
and resourceful and we've 26 years of experience
and knowledge of consumer facing design. We work
in partnership with both national and international
brands across a wide range of market sectors.

## Expertise
Identity
Communications
Environment
Merchandising
Packaging
Exhibitions
Consultancy

## Clients
Audi, Bentley Motors, Boots, California Academy of
Sciences, Comet, Design Council, Dunhill, George at
ASDA (Walmart), Hammersons (Bullring Development),
Henri-Lloyd, HSBC, KFC, Kohler Mira, Ladybird, Levi
Strauss, Marks & Spencer, Mobiltel, Ozwald Boateng,
Roland, Sony Computer Entertainment, Sony
Electronics, Thorntons, Timberland Boot Company,
Truworths, Virgin Megastores, WGSN.

## Awards
Future Marketing Awards 2006
Levi's Revolution – Best Use of Retail

Chain Store Age Awards 2005
Timberland Boot Company Store – International
Category

POPAI Europe Awards 2005
Sony PSP Sampling – Leisure, Electronics,
Hi-Fi & Video Category

Marketing Design Awards 2005
Boots No7 – Sales Promotion & Point of Purchase
Category

**See also Interior, Retail and Event Design p. 168**

1 'Roland Planet', Retail Graphic Identity
2 Thorntons 'Art of the Chocolatier' Brand Language
3 Levi's Kids Brand Identity
4 Levi's Brand Photography
5 Levi's 'Revolution' Packaging
6 KFC Brand Language and Packaging

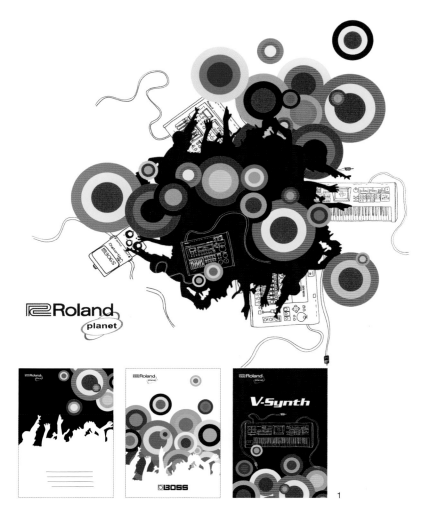

1

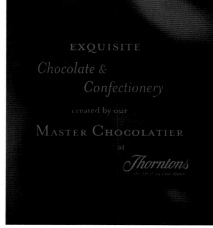

2

3

4

5

6

# Clusta Ltd

31-41 Bromley Street / Birmingham B9 4AN
T +44 (0)121 604 0004 / F +44 (0)121 604 3344
hello@clusta.com
www.clusta.com

**Management** Matthew Clugston, Russell Townsend
**Contact** Andrew Bowyer
**Staff** 14 **Founded** 1997

Clusta is home to a collective of the finest designers working with some of the world's biggest brands and quirkiest independents.

We work in all media across print, web and video to produce original, engaging identities and groundbreaking design.

We make our clients look good...and they love us for it!

**Our Services**
Branding
Graphic Design
Illustration
Character Design
Video & Post Production
Web & Flash Design
Disco Dancing
Photography
3D Modelling

**Our Clients**
Helix
Carphone Warehouse
Amnesty International
Channel 4
Orange
Pacha Group
Defected Records
Glue London
RPM Ltd
Agency.com
Tibbatts Associates

**See also New Media Design p. 136 and our sister company ClustaSpace in New Media Design p. 138**

01_Back To Mine: Adam Freeland - DMC
CD artwork

02_Back To Mine: Roots Manuva - DMC
CD artwork

Clusta

03_**For The Love Of House** Volume 1 - Defected
Design concept and CD artwork

04_**For The Love Of House** Volume 2 - Defected
Design concept and CD artwork

05,06_**InTheDetail**
Detail of DM marketing piece featuring brand ident

07_**Ten4 Magazine** Issue 3
Cover Design for Channel 4's creative network magazine

05

06

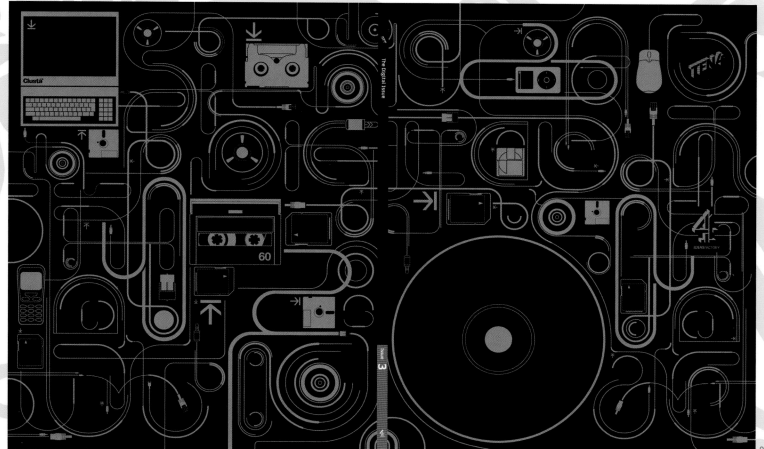

07

# Enigma Creative Solutions Ltd
## Sharper by Design

119-120 High Street / Eton SL4 6AN / Berkshire
T +44 (0)1753 496 470 / F +44 (0)1753 496 482
dominic.softly@enigmaCS.com
www.enigmaCS.com

**Management** Richard Pryer, Alan Surman,
Dominic Softly **Contact** Dominic Softly
**Staff** 21 **Founded** 1987

Multiple award-winning.

Reliable.

Adaptable.

Intelligent.

Creative.

From initial brief to your ROI, we deliver on
exhibitions, events, video production, new media,
websites & print – and all points between.

Enigma look at the big picture and the telling detail.
Result? End-to-end solutions. Globally. Think of us
as a Creative Intelligence Agency. (The other CIA).

"Everything should be made as simple as possible,
but not simpler." Albert Einstein

**Selected Clients**
Adobe
Airbus
British Airways
British Telecom
Compaq
DTI
Fiat
Indesit
Intel
Mobil
National Lottery
Orange
Philips
QinetiQ
Royal Mail
Shell
Siemens
BSkyB
Sony UK
Sun
Royal Navy
Toshiba
Ubisoft
Union Bank of Switzerland
Virgin Atlantic

**See also Interior, Retail and Event Design p. 174**

1   Party & Live Entertainment
2   Trade Show Environment
3   Branding & Design
4   Interior
5   New Product Launch, Exhibition & POS
6   Theatre & Live Action
7   Product Launch & Content
8   Immersive Showroom
9   Video
10  Print & New Media
11  Interactive Museum Experience

PORSCHE DESIGN

5

8

9

7

10

11

# Enterprise IG
## The Global Brand Agency

11-33 St John Street / London EC1M 4PJ
T +44 (0)20 7559 7000 / F +44 (0)20 7559 7001
info@enterpriseig.com
www.enterpriseig.co.uk

**Contact** John Mathers, UK CEO
**Founded** 1976

Enterprise IG is one of the world's leading
international brand agencies that has the resource of
nearly 600 people, covering 22 offices in 20 countries.

Enterprise IG believes that great companies and their
brands are built on a Compelling Truth™. A truth so
powerful it is transformational – building preference
and differentiation with consumers, customers and
employees. At Enterprise IG we partner with our
clients to find the Compelling Truth™ that underpins
their company, product or service brands.

We provide first-class Strategy, Design and
Engagement advice to major multinational and local
blue-chip clients. Our extensive range of skills and
experience, engaging both internal and external
audiences, ensures that the Compelling Truth™ is
delivered at all touch points – from identity, brand
architecture and communications through packaging,
product design, POS, brand language, retail
manifestation, brand experience, brand environment,
live events and interactive media.

**See also Packaging Design p. 108,**
**New Media Design p. 142 and Interior, Retail**
**and Event Design p. 176**

CREDIT SUISSE

# Felton Communication
## effective design

2 Bleeding Heart Yard / London EC1N 8SJ
T +44 (0)20 7405 0900 / F +44 (0)20 7430 1550
design@felton.co.uk
www.feltoncom.com

**Management** Roger Felton, Kate Hall
**Contact** Juliette Mauve
**Staff** 10 **Founded** 1989 **Memberships** DBA, CSD

### Company Profile
Creating truly effective brand identities and visual
communications for large and small organisations in
both the private and public sector for over 16 years.
Our approach is straightforward. Our creativity is
logically lateral. Our work works.

### Clients
BAA (airport property)
Terrence Higgins Trust (Sexual health)
Walk to School (UK national campaign)
NHS (health)
Lambeth Council (local Authority)
Lovells (law)
Family Mosaic (housing)
Sutton and East Surrey Water (utility)
TMA (cross cultural training)
MDU/DDU (medical defence)
Yarrow (learning disabilities)
Adidas (sportswear)

Identity for a UK
distribution and storage
warehouse developer.

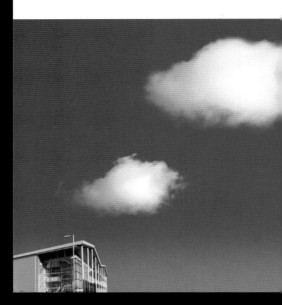

VOLUM∃

Brand identity and promotional
material for housing association
**Family Mosaic.**

Identity and campaign for **Living Streets'** national 'Walk to School' campaign in UK targeting primary schools.

Corporate and sales literature for UK airport property specialists **BAA Lynton**, including 'bigger thinking' campaign.

Lambeth

Brand custodians for Europe's largest sexual health charity.

Brand identity and numerous intergrated campaigns for a London local authority.

CHAPS men's sexual health conference ident, managed by **Terrence Higgins Trust**.

FELTON

# Fitch

121-141 Westbourne terrace / London W2 6JR
T +44 (0)20 7479 0900 / F +44 (0)20 7479 0600
david.balko@fitch.com
www.fitch.com

**Management** Rodney Fitch (wordwide), Lucy Unger,
Tim Greenhlagh (London) **Contact** David Balko
**Staff** 80 **Founded** 1972 **Memberships** D&AD, ISTD,
CSD, DBA

## Company Profile
Fitch is one of the world's best known and most
influential design agencies. Fitch has a unique focus
on retailing in all its forms, and is expert in designing
consumer brands and retail environments.

Fitch has over 450 associates in 18 different studios
across 11 countries working across time zones to
retail the goods, services and personalities of our
clients all over the world.

## Brand Communications
Fitch are designers, but we like to think of ourselves
as storytellers. Fitch see each new challenge as a
story in need of writing and telling. Creating a
persuasive design message is similar to writing a play,
poem or story. It's the brand as narrative – punctuated
for sense, meaning and effect – taking the brand and
the consumer on a structured journey that is both
logical and emotional.

Fitch is helping to write new chapters in brands'
histories, defining the character and personality
of those brands. For the brand to be a hero to
the consumer we need to understand its strengths,
weaknesses, habits, values and attitudes: all of
which are interpreted differently and evolve and
mature with time.

Fitch think about locations for the story. The choice
of setting, the spirit of place, can make or break
a character and render any story unbelievable
or confusing.

Only when these elements are in place do Fitch put
pen to paper, using symbols, typography, images,
words, colour and form to create our narrative and
bring our stories to life.

Fitch will continue to work with brands to explore new
settings and plot developments. Fitch will create
stories that are simple, memorable and engaging. This
is how tales are handed down, how a brand endures
and evolves with each new interpretation and delivery
of the story.

For Fitch, brand communications is about so
much more than design. Fitch craft stories that
communicate the core values and personality of
the brand. Fitch mission is to set the mood, distil
emotions and tell your story in the most imaginative,
compelling and memorable way possible.

## Clients Include
Vodafone
Nokia
BAT
Carhartt
Amsterdam Schiphol Airport
2006 Doha Asian Games
Yum brands
DSG
Goodyear Dunlop
Lego
Harrods
Hyundai
Russian Post
Microsoft
Central Food halls

**See also Interior, Retail and Event Design p. 178**

01

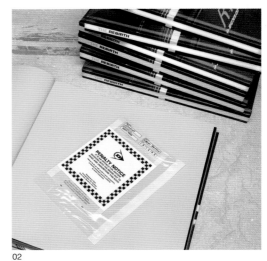

02

03

04

05

06

**DUNLOP BRAND RELAUNCH**
01 Motorsport sponsorship communication
02 Dunlop brand book
07 Brand language photographic style

**15TH ASIAN GAMES DOHA 2006**
03 Special edition mascot stamps
04 Qatar Airways mascot livery

**KELVINGROVE ART GALLERY AND MUSEUM**
05 New brand identity
**AQUASCUTUM**
06 Flagship store design

# Fluid
## Visual Communications

Fluid Studios / 12 Tenby Street / Birmingham B1 3AJ
T +44 (0)121 212 0121 / F +44 (0)121 212 0202
drop@fluidesign.co.uk
www.fluidesign.co.uk

**Management** James Glover, Neil Roddis
**Contacts** James Glover, Barny Morris
**Founded** 1995

**Company Profile**
Design/Branding/Advertising/Multimedia/Web/
Exhibition/Packaging

From brand identity to ad campaigns; from 3D
modelling to exhibitions; from packaging to web
design – Fluid employ a strategic approach and
progressive design to create a concept that will fulfil
all your requirements. Whether you need a universal
vision or unique attitude to an individual project,
Fluid's comprehensive knowledge and experience
ensure successful solutions at every level.

**Clients Include**
Adidas – Pursuit Marketing
BBC Worldwide
Capcom Europe
Coco-Cola
Diageo
Eidos
Electronic Arts
EMI Records
Fierce Earth
Levi's – Slice PR
Microsoft Xbox
Nivea/Beiersdorf
Parlophone
Sony Computer Entertainment Europe
T-26 Digital Type Foundry
THQ
UbiSoft
UK Film Council

1  Fluid 10 years' work compilation 1995-2006

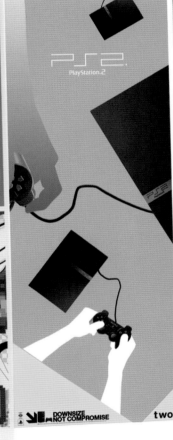

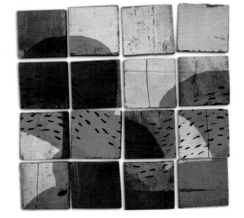

CHOP TILL YOU DROP

DEADRISING

CAPTIV8

British design 2006-2007

FIERCE
19th may - 3rd june
www.fiercetv.co.uk
06
the international performance festival that bites

800.
851.7784.

the birds

FLUID

# The Formation Creative Consultants Ltd

59 Charlotte Road / London EC2A 3QW
T +44 (0)20 7739 8198 / F +44 (0)20 7729 1950
akilby@theformation-cc.co.uk
www.theformation-cc.co.uk

**Management** Adrian Kilby **Contact** Adrian Kilby
**Staff** 4 **Memberships** D&AD, STD

The Formation first took to the skies on 1 August 1994 under the command of Adrian Kilby – designer and reincarnated fighter pilot!

We describe ourselves as creative consultants and specialise in brand building. Our expertise is international and spans corporate identity, print, retail interiors, exhibition, packaging and website design. We also have a portfolio of advertising work, undertaken on behalf of the clients.

Our approach is personal and respectful, yet thorough and stimulating. We challenge our clients in the same way we expect to be challenged ourselves.

We are responsible for a number of the UK's leading entrepreneurial brands and are the specialists in ethical packaging, having developed the world's first fully biodegradable sandwich pack with our clients foo·go. Our work is regularly selected for publication and the company has won awards both in the UK and overseas.

1-2 The Hoxton Urban Lodge, luxury budget hotel – branding, print, interior detailing, advertising and website design
3 Spianata, Roman bakery – packaging, print and interior design
4 Stanfords, the world's largest map and travel bookshop – branding, interior graphics, packaging and print
5 foo·go, innovative food retailer – branding, packaging, print and website design
6 Glamorous Amorous, chic lingerie boutique – branding, packaging, print, advertising and website design

46

THE HOXTON
URBAN LODGE
• • •

everybody's happy
www.babaloo.co.uk

we are what you eat
foo·go™

wannaburger
irresistible burgers and shakes

GLAMOROUS
AMOROUS.COM
CHIC LINGERIE BOUTIQUE

2

poet in the city

# Hemisphere
## Design and Marketing Consultants

Binks Building / 30-32 Thomas Street /
Northern Quarter / Manchester M4 1ER
T +44 (0)161 907 3730 / F +44 (0)161 907 3731
post@hemispheredmc.com
www.hemispheredmc.com

**Management** Grant Windridge, Sue Vanden
**Contacts** Grant Windridge, Sue Vanden
**Staff** 9 **Founded** 1988
**Memberships** New York Type Directors Club, DBA

### Company Profile

Hemisphere devises creative, intelligent and practical solutions to branding, promotional and communications challenges, each developed by combining quality of thought and quality of execution.

We bring over 18 years of experience to projects ranging from strategic branding and identity design through design for print and web to exhibition and environmental design. Our ability to deliver well-crafted and thought-through solutions to complex and wide-reaching identity issues has led to a number of high profile projects in place branding and in the public sector.

Whatever the size or scope of the problem, all projects are tackled with the ingenuity, craft and attention to detail that are the hallmarks of Hemisphere's work.

### Clients

The Bridgewater Hall
Imperial War Museum North
Marketing Manchester
Royal Northern College of Music
Urbis
Destination Manchester Ltd
Groundwork
Manchester City Council
Sunderland
Bolton
Salford City Council
Mersey Basin Campaign
Tate Liverpool
Financial Times
Sustainability Northwest
Northwest Development Agency
North East Assembly

1 Summer of Love exhibition and promotional material, Tate Liverpool
2 Destination and council brand for the UK's largest town, Bolton
3 Against The Odds – The Story of Bomber Command, design of exhibition and marketing materials, Imperial War Museum North
4 Destination and associated brands for the city of Sunderland
5 Residents magazine, Olympic Pool naming and advertising campaign, Children's Services marketing materials, Sunderland City Council

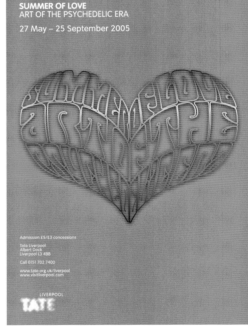

1

4

2

3

5

# Kemistry

43 Charlotte Road / London EC2A 3PD
T +44 (0)20 7729 3636 / F +44 (0)20 7749 2760
info@kemistry.co.uk
www.kemistry.co.uk

**Management** Graham McCallum, Richard Churchill
**Contact** Guy Hewitt
**Staff** 15 **Founded** 1996
**Memberships** D&AD, Promax & BDA

## Company Profile

We develop, create and manage brand identities
for use across all media platforms.

Whether launching new or refreshing existing
identities, we have significant international experience
and a first class track record in helping brand owners
engage with their audiences and realise their potential.

As a team, we are passionate about what we do.
Creativity remains at the forefront of every project we
undertake. We give clients clarity of voice with brand
solutions that encompass on and off-screen media,
reaching corporate and consumer targets.

Market dynamics, such as shifting audience
behaviour, emerging competitive pressures and media
diversification, are forcing brands to evolve or die.
Kemistry tracks these dynamics to improve forward
vision and create genuinely strategic design solutions.

Our work has been recognised with many
international creative and design effectiveness
awards. The company recently received a Queen's
Award for Enterprise recognising outstanding
achievement in international trade.

### Recent Clients

ABC Plus Media SA
Cathay Pacific Airways
Channel 4 – FilmFour
CNN International
Delia On-line
Digital Bridge
Discovery Networks Europe
Duna Televizio
Independent Sports Network
KLM
MTV3
National Geographic Channel
NRK
Publieke Omroep
Shoreditch Trust
News Corporation
The Scottish Office
TV4
Vue Entertainment
Zone Media

1  Zone Media – brand creation, on-screen channel
   identity and sales and marketing materials
2  Digital Bridge – brand creation, sales and
   marketing material and interactive sub brand
   identity
3  Nederland 1 2 & 3 – rebrand and identity creation
   for Dutch public broadcaster
4  From left to right: Duna – on-screen brand identity
   for Hungarian state broadcaster, Duna news
   package CNNI, strategic brand repositioning TV4
   Sweden, on-screen identity for main channel,
   TV4+ brand creation and on-screen identity MTV3
   Finland, brand repositioning and on-screen identity

1

2

**ɪone**
**omantica**

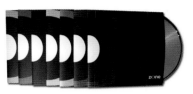

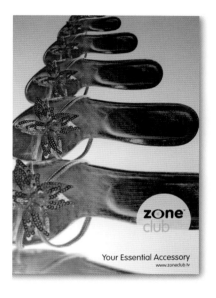

3

4

# Kino Design

Smokehouse Yard / 44-46 St John Street /
London EC1M 4DF
T +44 (0)20 7490 5850
andrew@kinodesign.com
www.kinodesign.com

**Contacts** Andrew Bignell and Andy Stanfield
**Staff** 10 **Founded** 1985

Let's keep this simple. Kino Design is an independent
consultancy that creates clear, strong and highly-effective
design and communication solutions. Our approach?
We listen, we ask questions, we challenge and then,
most importantly, we get on with it – and that's the truth.

We specialise in:

**Brand Identity**
Creating new brands
Expanding and refreshing existing brands
Brand implementation

**Strategic**
Communications planning
Change management
Employee communications

**Print Design**
Marketing material
Developing literature systems
Promotional literature

**Clients**
Visa
Sodexho
Aberdeen Asset Management
Booz Allen Hamilton
CNBC
Derbyshire Building Society
JPMorgan
Sirva
Barclays
Pickfords
ODPM
DCLG
GE Capital
Dalai Lama

1  London 2012
   – logo, brand identity and guidelines
2  Financial Services Skills Council
   – marketing communications
3  Academy for Sustainable Communities
   – logo, brand identity and guidelines
4  Insight Investment
   – brand identity and guidelines
5  The truth books
   – discover the shocking truth about design
   agencies and branding
6  Street League charity
   – logo, brand identity and guidelines

1

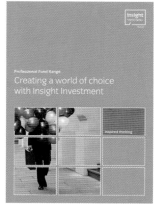

**Strength in numbers**

Financial Services
Skills Council

**Strength in numbers**

Financial Services
Skills Council

**Strength in numbers**

Financial Services
Skills Council

**Strength in numbers**

Financial Services
Skills Council

**Strength in numbers**

Financial Services
Skills Council

2

Professional Fund Range
Creating a world of choice
with Insight Investment

Aim for higher returns
with lower levels of risk

Leading fund managers
brought together for you

4

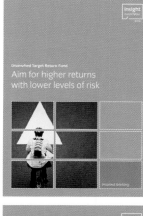

**asc** Academy for
Sustainable
Communities

Sustainable Communities:
Environmental

Sustainable Communities:

Sustainable Communities:
Well connected

Sustainable Communities:
Well designed

Sustainable Communities:
Fair for everyone

Sustainable Communities:
Well served

Sustainable Communities:
Well run

Sustainable Communities:
Thriving

3

**The truth
about
design
agencies**

**The truth
about
branding**

**The sofa check**

**Beware of the design agency
with too many sofas.**

If they're for the designers to
relax in, they clearly aren't
working hard enough.

If they're for you to sit in, then
expect to be kept waiting a
long time while they finish
your work.

5

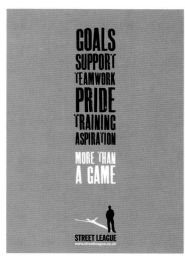

**GOALS
SUPPORT
TEAMWORK
PRIDE
TRAINING
ASPIRATION**

**MORE THAN
A GAME**

STREET LEAGUE
www.streetleague.co.uk

**GOAL**

Training

6

# La Boca

231 Portobello Road / London W11 1LT
T +44 (0)20 7792 9791 / F +44 (0)20 7792 9871
eatme@laboca.co.uk
www.laboca.co.uk

**Management** Scot Bendall, Alain de la Mata
**Contact** Scot Bendall
**Staff** 4 **Founded** 2002

**Putting the Ape into Apricot**
La Boca is an independent design circus specializing in highly original art & design for the film, music and fashion industries.

Our work ranges from limited edition vinyl record sleeves to full scale media campaigns, and our twisted touch has left its indelible mark on projects for a wide range of international clients.

**Clients**
Amelia's Magazine
Artificial Eye
BAC Films
DC Recordings
Kickin Records
LoDown Magazine
Muse Films
Nookii
Pan-Européenne
Sony BMG
Studio Ghibli
Visible Noise
Wild Bunch

1   Kelpe, 12" album, DC Recordings
2   Bullet For My Valentine, international album and singles campaign, Sony BMG
3   The Emperor Machine, 12" single, DC Recordings
4   Three Times, UK theatrical campaign, Artificial Eye
5   Daft Punk – Interstella 5555, international marketing brochure, BAC Films
6   Innocence, UK theatrical campaign, Artificial Eye
7   Innocence, UK DVD, Artificial Eye
8   Forbidden Fruit
9   Howl's Moving Castle, international marketing brochure, Studio Ghibli
10  A New Life, festival poster, Wild Bunch
11  Lostprophets, UK album campaign, Visible Noise
12  Amelia's Magazine, Issue 2
13  Irreversible, brand and international marketing brochure, Wild Bunch
14  Tom Tyler, 12" album, DC Recordings
15  The Emperor Machine, 12" single, DC Recordings
16  Bullet For My Valentine, promotional stickers, Sony BMG
17  Kelpe, 12" single, DC Recordings

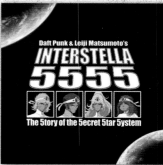

"A **boldly original** take on a story by Frank Wedekind." *THE TIMES*

"**Bewitchingly strange...** Buñuel meets Angela Carter meets Enid Blyton" *INDEPENDENT ON SUNDAY*

"The **most remarkable** cinema debut of recent times." Nick James. SIGHT AND SOUND

A FILM BY
LUCILE HADZIHALILOVIC

# innocence

WINNER
BEST FILM

WINNER
BEST NEW DIRECTOR

MARION COTILLARD · HÉLÈNE DE FOUGEROLLES · ZOÉ AUCLAIR · LÉA BRIDAROLLI · BÉRANGÈRE HAUBRUGE · ALISON LALIEUX · OLGA PEYTAVI-MULLER

6

innocence

A FILM BY
LUCILE HADZIHALILOVIC

7

8

HOWL'S
MOVING CASTLE

9

# A NEW LIFE
PHILIPPE GRANDRIEUX

10

# LOSTPROPHETS

NOBIS · PRO LEMMA · VOBIS

*Liberation Transmission*
## THE NEW ALBUM
RELEASED 26.06.06
FEATURING THE HIT SINGLE 'ROOFTOPS'

WWW.LOSTPROPHETS.COM

11

12

IRREVERSIBLE

13

TOM TYLER
FORWARD
GOING
BACKWARDS

14

EMPEROR
MACHINE

15

16

17

# Linney Design

Adamsway / Mansfield / Nottinghamshire NG18 4FW
T +44 (0)1623 450 470 / F +44 (0)1623 450 471
solutions@linney.com
www.linney.com

**Company Profile**

A design company? Well, we're absolutely passionate
about design and have been for over twenty years.
So, yes, we're a design company. But we don't
want to mislead you, there's so much more to us
than just design.

Drop into our offices and you're as likely to hear
discussions about brand strategy and customer
relationship marketing with our clients as you are
about design.

We're helping our clients all over the world to realise
the potential of their brands and their businesses,
not just through superb design but through informed
creative direction and brand consultation.

Open the door to our offices and you'll see more
than 50 passionate designers, programmers,
managers and experts in all media – providing
and sharing the knowledge vital to our success
and our clients' longevity.

So of course we're passionate about design –
but only by combining this passion with insightful
market knowledge and great business sense do
we ensure we are providing the right design solutions
for our clients.

**Expertise**

Strategic Marketing
Brand Management
Graphic Design
Digital Marketing & Strategy
Digital Creative
Print
Distribution

# design is alive in mansfield

Yes, one of the UK's largest design businesses is based in the small town of Mansfield. We find it conveniently located at the centre of the world. It helps when working with global brands.

LINNEY design

design is alive in mansfield sherwood forest CenterParcs munich united kingdom POST OFFICE holland hamamatsu and a place near you

# Lisa Tse Ltd
## Creative Digital Branding

56 Frith Street / Soho / London W1D 3JG
T +44 (0)20 7168 9460 / F +44 (0)20 7990 9460
design@lisatse.com
www.lisatse.com

**Management** Lisa Tse, Creative Director
**Contact** Lisa Tse
**Staff** 4 **Membership** British Design Initiative

**Company Profile**
With a focus on fresh perspectives and forward
thinking, Lisa Tse Ltd adopts a creatively driven
approach that supports companies in a diverse
commercial capacity.

Our studio provides a multidisciplinary design service
harnessing pure design with thoughtful intelligent
details.

**Expertise**
Branding and Graphics
Illustration
Packaging
Web Design
Copywriting

**Clients**
Checkland Kindleysides
Manjoh.com
Mews of Mayfair
Plan
Preen by Thornton & Bregazzi
Scott Wilson
Sidhu & Simon
Simpsons of Cornhill PLC
Zubio Incorporated

**Awards**
iF International Forum Communication Design
Award 2004
American Design Award for Web & Graphic
Design 2004
D&AD & Nesta Product Design & Innovation
Award 2003

**Weblinks**
www.mewsofmayfair.com
www.scottwilsonlondon.com
www.sidhuandsimon.com
www.plan-design.co.uk

1   Laser cut invitations
2   Matchbox tents form an architectural line
    of rooftops
3   Matchbox tent open
4   Folding business cards
5   Mens washroom incorporates branded signage
    and features large scale photography for a glass
    urinal. Industrial Design by James Williamson.

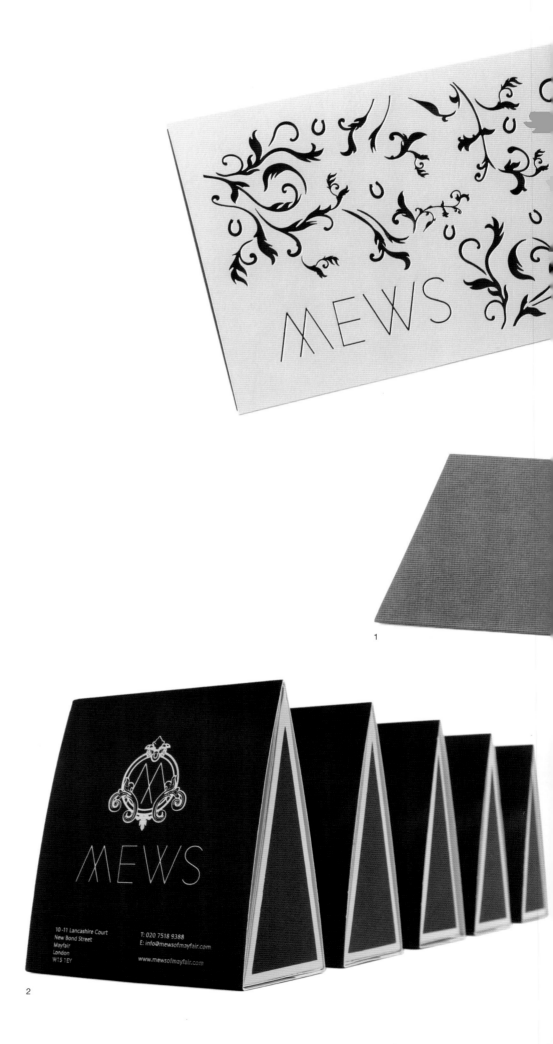

HOW DO YOU DO

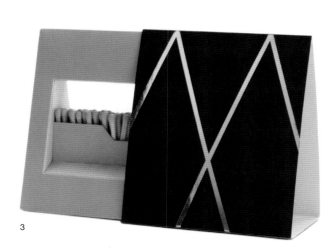

3

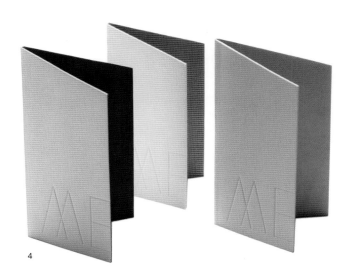

4

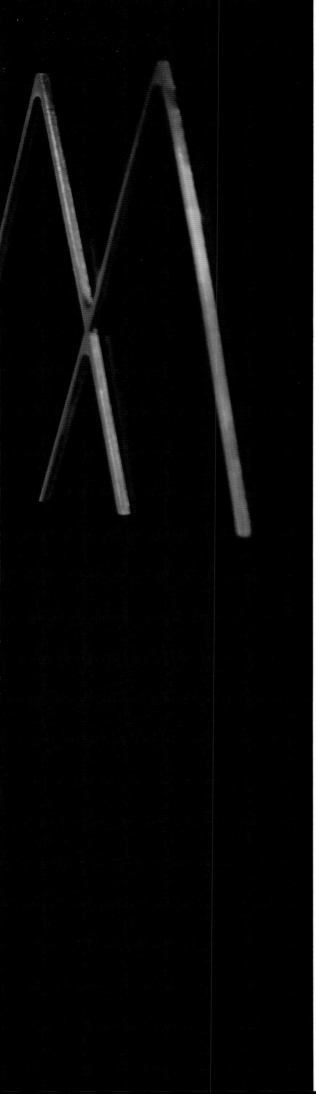

"Lisa's creative vision and commercial acumen are the perfect complement for any business. She is a true inspiration whose attention to detail, instinctive talent and creative flair exceeds expectations time and time again."

**James Robson, Founder, Mews of Mayfair**

## lisa tse
CREATIVE DIGITAL BRANDING

WWW.LISATSE.COM

# Lloyd Northover

2 Goodge Street / London W1T 2QA
T +44 (0)20 7420 4850 / F +44 (0)20 7420 4858
trudi.osborne@lloydnorthover.com
www.lloydnorthover.com

**Contacts** Trudi Osborne, Jim Bodoh, Mike Taylor
**Founded** 1975 **Memberships** DBA, D&AD, CBI,
CSD, IOD, RSA, IIID, BDI, The Design Council,
The Marketing Society, Sign Design Society

## We create value by transforming how people feel about your business

The success of your organisation depends on the
connections you make with the people that matter –
your staff, your customers and your other valued
stakeholders. It's not just what they think about your
business, but how they feel about it that really
matters.

That's why the right brand, delivered in the right way,
is crucial.

We will work with you to discover, define, design
and deliver your brand, wherever and however
people experience your organisation – transforming
how people feel about your business through not
only your brand, but also your communications,
your people and your environments.

### Our services include:
Brand strategy
Brand identity
Brand management
Digital communications
Marketing communications
Corporate communications
Internal communications
Advertising
Public relations
Retail strategy
Visual merchandising
Point of purchase/point of sale
Experiential marketing
Architecture
Signing and wayfinding
Brand experience
Brand environment
Organisational engagement
People development

If you like what you see, get in touch to find out what
we've done for others and, more importantly, what we
can do for you.

### See also New Media Design p. 144

1 Arts & Business corporate brochure
2 Thames Valley University brand identity
3 7C (an e-CRM business) brand book
4 National Savings and Investments website –
   winner of DBA Design Effectiveness Award 2005
5 University of Manchester brand architecture
6 Euronext advertising campaign
7 SAAB brand experience design
8 Lexus brand experience and environment design

1

4

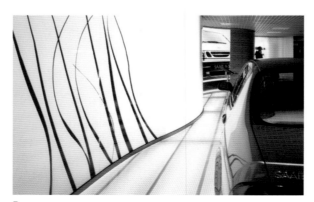

7

8

Thames Valley University
London Reading Slough

Thames Valley University
London Reading Slough

Thames Valley University
London Reading Slough

2

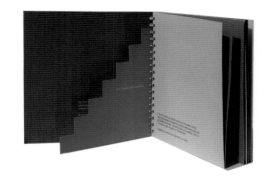

3

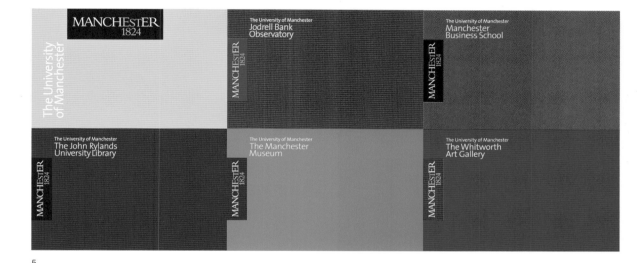

5

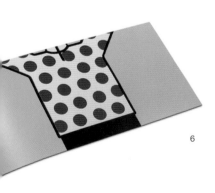

6

Lloyd
Northover

# NE6 Design Consultants

4 St James Terrace / Newcastle upon Tyne NE1 4NE
T +44 (0)191 221 2606 / F +44 (0)191 221 2607
info@ne6design.co.uk
www.ne6design.co.uk

**Management** Jeremy Royle, David Coates
**Contacts** Jeremy Royle, David Coates
**Staff** 9 **Founded** 1977

### History

Established in 1997, NE6 has 9 members employed
in its Newcastle upon Tyne studio. NE6 Design
Consultants provides design services for major UK
clients and is driven by creativity, innovation, client
satisfaction and excellence.

### Approach

Good design starts with a good ear. Funny to think
that it's sound that sparks such a quintessentially
visual means of communication as design. But, as
far as we are concerned, that's where it all begins,
with the voice of our clients.

A good ear-bending is always the first step to
producing design that gets tongues wagging.
The better we listen, the better we understand.
And the better we can shape a strategy and define
a direction together. Only then do we put pen, pencil
or marker to paper. Or, indeed, hand to mouse.

The dialogue doesn't stop there however. Throughout
the whole design process we relish close contact with
our clients because it's an integral part of developing
solutions we can all be proud of.

Two good ears are better than one. What lies between
them is what we hope to apply to our client's vision.

### Awards

NE6 has collected creative awards from New York,
Paris, Barcelona, London, Glasgow and Manchester.
NE6 has also been recognised as one of the top 50
graphic design organisations in the UK, in a creative
survey carried out by Design Week.

1 Beaverbrooks the Jewellers
2 Alex Telfer Photography
3 Barnardo's
4 Mayborn Group
5 Sage UK Ltd
6 Midland Mainline

1

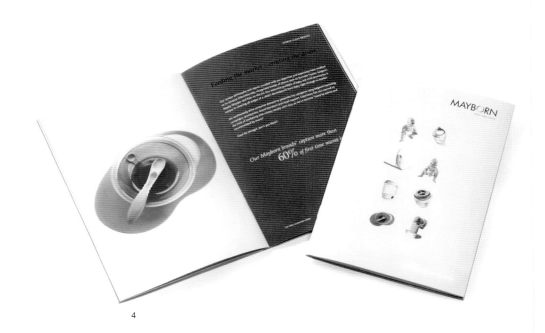

4

2

3

5

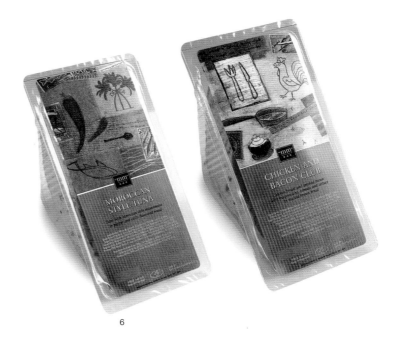

6

# Parent
## Brand Design & Art Direction

Bristol & West House / Post Office Road /
Bournemouth BH1 1BL
T +44 (0)1202 311 711
mail@parentdesign.co.uk
www.parentdesign.co.uk

### Company Profile
Parent is a creative boutique based on the sunny
south coast. Specialising in design and art direction
for print, web and brand identity our clients range
from small fashion labels to large corporates, record
labels and ad agencies.

# pi global

1 Colville Mews / Lonsdale Road / London W11 2AR
T +44 (0)20 7908 0808 / F +44 (0)20 7908 0809
hello@piglobal.com
www.piglobal.com

**Management** Don Williams, CEO
**Contacts** Vanessa Lumby, Client Services Director;
Pia Badziong, Marketing and Research Manager
**Staff** 60 **Founded** 1984

### Company Profile
Founded in 1984, pi global are an independent
branding, visual brand id application and packaging
design consultancy. We operate out of our Notting Hill
offices in London with international, multi-disciplinary
teams.

pi global's fundamental passion is 'iconistic® brand
id' – our branding methodology and core philosophy,
the focus of which is the optimisation of our clients'
investment in communication and the long term
health and growth of the brands we work on – our
aim is always to provide vastly improved saliency
and facilitation of stretch and growth for our clients'
brands.

We specialise in all areas of FMCG and Healthcare
branding, id application and packaging design.
From billion dollar Global brands to 'local jewels' –
we have created, strengthened and protected
many of the world's most recognised, long lasting
and commercially successful brand identities.

As well as brand strategy, planning, design,
stewardship and implementation, pi global offer
our clients a wide range of disciplines through our
specialist divisions: brand ideation and innovation
through pid8 – consumer and retail observation and
analysis as well as 'real-world' research consultancy
through picu – structural design, engineering,
production and prototyping through pi3.

We are passionate about brands – we will not work
on private label products/pseudo brands. We
measure our performance in four ways: the longevity
of our client relationships, the longevity of our visual
brand foundations, the commercial success of
our work, and the value of the brands in our portfolio.

### Services Include
Brand Strategy; Brand Naming; Brand and
Technical Futures; iconistic® Brand Id; Visual
Brand Architecture; Visual Brand Audit; New Brand
Development (nbd); New Product Development
(npd); Pack Graphic Design; Pack structural
Design; Structural Packaging Innovation; Prototype
Development; Management of Tooling, Development
and Sourcing; Consumer/retail observation and
analysis; Research Consultancy; Production
Consultancy; Technical Management; Brand
Stewardship; Marcomms.

### Clients Include
Procter & Gamble; Twinings; Bayer Healthcare;
Masterfoods Europe; Akzo Nobel; Carlsberg; Arla;
Reckitt Benckiser.

**See also Packaging Design p. 116**

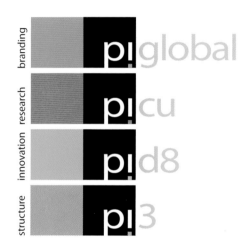

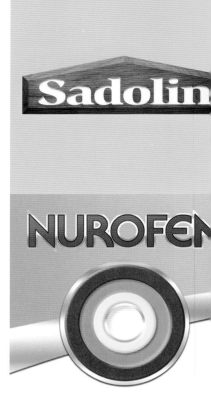

 Oilatum

 TWININGS OF London

 Rennie

 MilkyWay

 blink™

mrs Crimble's

 Olli

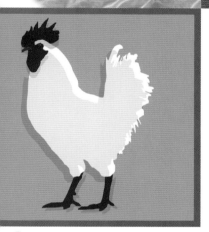

PRO PLUS®

 h&s head & shoulders

nicorette®

 תלמה

 TL ANGETWINS

International®

 pl

# +Prism.Brand.Architects

The Greenhouse / 521 Gibb Street /
Birmingham B9 4AA / Midlands
T +44 (0)121 224 8270 / T +44 (0)794 924 8602
ben@prismbrandarchitects.com
www.prismbrandarchitects.com

**Management** Benjamin Ridgway
**Contact** Benjamin Ridgway
**Staff** 3 Founded 1999

**Brand influence – We understand it, we breed it, you need it.**

+Prism.Brand.Architects, will construct a brand communication that projects your aspirations, and will capture your audience both visually and strategically. We +build brands from infancy or +energise existing brands which are in need of new and fresh ideas to communicate a project. Already we have created many effective brand identities. We are working with our existing clients to foresee the future of their brands and advising the most effective ways to +expose them creatively to their market.

**+Prism Brand Services**

**+Build**
Brand creation
Brand communication/application
Marketing plans for infant brands
Market research

**+Energise**
Re-Brands
Advertising
Brochure design
Literature design
Email marketing
Website design

**+Expose**
Mail-shot design
Environmental advertising
Viral marketing
Launch events
PR

**Build+Energise+Expose**

+BUILD.
+ENERGISE.
+EXPOSE

+PRISM.BRAND.ARCHITECTS

+EXPOSE
BRAND.MARKETING

+ENERGISE
BRAND.EVOLUTION

+BUILD
BRAND.CREATION

# Rareform London
## Branding & Design Consultancy

First Floor / 148 Curtain Road / London EC2A 3AR
T +44 (0)20 7754 5962 / F +44 (0)20 7681 3150
sales@rareformlondon.com
www.rareformlondon.com

**Contact** Joe Hedges or Amy McHenry
**Membership** Chartered Society of Designers

### Company Profile
Award-winning, with excellent processes, unbeatable knowledge of design in varying cultures and yes, all our projects start from research and resulting strategy through to implementation across all channels... we also like to think all our work has something special – our clients certainly think so. Why not try us and see.

We cover the following areas and more; branding, print, web sites, intranet sites, pda, packaging, signage, wayfinding, forms, bills, dm, moving image, livery,...

### Clients
B&Q
BioPartners
BP
Central Saint Martins
Chapter 1
Church of England
Clifford Chance
Design Laboratory
EMAAR
Ernst & Young
Etisalat
Fibre Solutions
Freeserve
Home Bar
Horizon Life Care
Insights
Just Giving
Les Trois Garçons
M&S
Mobily
MTV
Mydeo
Osram
Perpetual Solutions
Psion
Raw Canvas
RDW
Royal Mail
Swiss Re
Tate
TFS
U:recruitment
Veropharm

BRANDING//
BRAND CONSULTATION//
PRINT//WEB//DIGITAL//
PACKAGING//
MOVING IMAGE//
IDEAS

**1** **ETISALAT** LIVERY FOR CORPORATE FLEET & PROMOTIONAL VEHICLES

**2** **ETISALAT** SIGNAGE & WAY FINDING FOR WHOLE OF UAE

**3** **ETISALAT** DESK TOPS AND SCREENSAVERS

**4** **ETISALAT** BRAND BOOK AND IDENTITY & BRAND GUIDELINES

**5** **ETISALAT** WEB SITE & ONLINE ADVERTISING

**6** **ETISALAT** RETAIL STORE BAGS

**7** **ETISALAT** SIM CARD PACKAGING

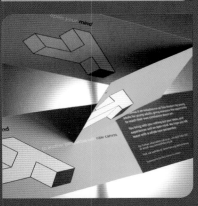

**RAREFORM**
Branding tomorrow

**1** **LES TROIS GARÇONS** PACKAGING FOR RESTAURANT

**2** **VEROPHARM** BRANDING FOR RUSSIAN PHARMACY

**3** **VEROPHARM** PACKAGING FOR RUSSIAN PHARMACY

**4** **LES TROIS GARÇONS** BRANDING & DESIGN FOR RESTAURANT (DW AWARD)

**5** **CHURCH OF ENGLAND** BRANDING & PACKAGING FOR LITURGY SOFTWARE

**6** **U:RECRUITMENT** BRANDING FOR NEW RECRUITMENT SPECIALISTS

**7** **ERNST & YOUNG** INTERNAL COMMUNICATIONS CAMPAIGN

**8** **TATE** BRANDING FOR YOUTH GROUP

**9** **MOBILY** BRANDING FOR SAUDI TELECOM

**10** **MOBILY** RETAIL DESIGN

**11** **MOBILY** PACKAGING FOR SIM CARD AND LITERATURE

**12** **TATE** PROMOTIONAL LITERATURE FOR YOUTH GROUP

**13** **CENTRAL SAINT MARTINS** BRANDING FOR DESIGN LABORATORY

**14** **MOBILY** DESIGN GUIDELINES

# Redpath

5 Gayfield Square / Edinburgh EH1 3NW
T +44 (0)131 556 9115 / F +44 (0)131 556 9116
redpath@redpath.co.uk
www.redpath.co.uk

**Management** Richard Irvine, Iain Lauder, Allison
Traynor **Contact** Richard Irvine
**Staff** 15 **Founded** 1995 **Memberships** DBA, D&AD,
BDI, RSA

## Company Profile

Redpath is a strategic creative agency of designers
and writers delivering truly joined-up communications.

We provide our clients with graphic design,
copywriting and brand consultancy services to deliver
complete and effective communication solutions for
their external and internal audiences.

Our work spans corporate & brand identities; printed
literature & annual reports; packaging & retail brand
experience; web & digital communications.

For every client, to every project, we bring passion,
vision and enthusiasm.

## Clients

ACE (Association of Consultants & Engineers)
Ben Dawson Furniture
British Council
Cave de Lugny Wines (Burgundy, France)
Cranfield School of Management
Edinburgh UNESCO City of Literature
Ethicon (part of Johnson & Johnson)
Glenfarclas Malt Whisky
HBOS plc
ICSC Europe
National Museums of Scotland
Skyparks
sportscotland
RBS Group
The Scottish Executive
The University of Edinburgh Management School

1  British Council: a feast of Film & Literature
   postcards
2  Cave de Lugny: Unité brand identity, packaging &
   website
3  sportscotland: Arena magazine
4  Ben Dawson Furniture: identity, marketing
   collateral, website

1

2

# Reinvigorate
## Total Brand Experience

2 Gads Hill / Trimmingham Road / Halifax HX2 7PX
T +44 (0)1422 340 055 / F +44 (0)1422 340 055
martin@reinvigorate.co.uk
www.reinvigorate.co.uk

**Contact** Martin Monks
**Staff** 12 plus specialist Project Managers
**Founded** 2003 **Memberships** Chartered Society
of Designers, Marketing Society

**Company Profile**
Reinvigorate deliver a total brand experience from
the creation and conception of the brand through
to the full brand experience in store. We have
the capabilities and expertise to deliver profitable
business and design solutions for any brand. Not only
do we design the brand experience we also Project
Manage the installation and construction of the full
retail environment within the client's specified budget.

**Clients**
Adams Childrenswear
Arkadia International
Boots Plc
Calderdale College
English Heritage
Fortunae Plc
Go Outdoors
Hallmark Cards Plc
H. Brown
Intimas Group Plc
Marks & Spencer Plc
Pearsons Group
Things International

**See also Interior, Retail and Event Design p. 186**

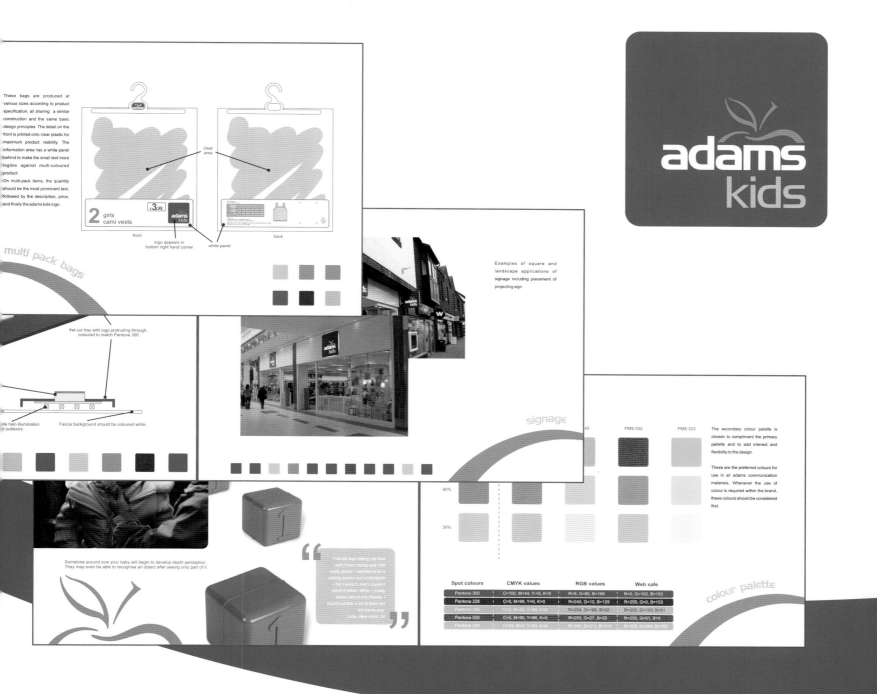

These bags are produced at various sizes according to product specification, all sharing a similar construction and the same basic design principles. The detail on the front is printed onto clear plastic for maximum product visibility. The information area has a white panel behind to make the small text more legible against multi-coloured product.

On multi-pack items, the quantity should be the most prominent text, followed by the description, price, and finally the adams kids logo.

clear area

2 girls cami vests

£3.99

adams kids

front

logo appears in bottom right hand corner

white panel

back

multi pack bags

fret cut tray with logo protruding through, coloured to match Pantone 300

Fascia background should be coloured white.

side halo illumination and outdoors.

Examples of square and landscape applications of signage including placement of projecting sign.

signage

PMS 032    PMS 333

60%

30%

The secondary colour palette is chosen to compliment the primary palette and to add interest and flexibility to the design.

These are the preferred colours for use in all adams communication materials. Whenever the use of colour is required within the brand, these colours should be considered first.

colour palette

Sometime around now your baby will begin to develop depth perception. They may even be able to recognise an object after seeing only part of it.

| Spot colours | CMYK values | RGB values | Web safe |
|---|---|---|---|
| Pantone 300 | C=100, M=44, Y=0, K=0 | R=9, G=90, B=166 | R=0, G=102, B=153 |
| Pantone 226 | C=0, M=99, Y=0, K=0 | R=240, G=10, B=129 | R=255, G=0, B=153 |
| Pantone 142 | C=0, M=36, Y=85, K=0 | R=254, G=166, B=32 | R=255, G=153, B=51 |
| Pantone 032 | C=0, M=90, Y=86, K=0 | R=253, G=27, B=20 | R=255, G=51, B=0 |
| Pantone 333 | C=43, M=0, Y=63, K=0 | R=146, G=211, B=174 | R=153, G=204, B=153 |

# things*

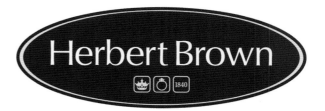

 Pearsons

# SCG London
## Brand Synergy™

8 Plato Place / 72-74 St Dionis Road /
London SW6 4TU
T +44 (0)20 7371 7522
susan@scglondon.uk.com
www.scglondon.co.uk

**Contacts** Clive Woodger, Susan Mark
**Staff** 15 **Founded** 1991

### Company Profile

SCG London is an international team based in
London providing creative strategy, design and
delivery for successful brand development. We
believe in the ability to understand, manage and work
with key media and processes which contribute to a
successful brand image, profile and user experience.

We work internationally and in the U.K. and the
success of our multi-disciplined approach is reflected
in the calibre and profile of our clients.

We combine coordinated strategic and marketing
skills with the effective design and alignment of
corporate identity development, architecture, interiors,
graphics, merchandising, point of sale, packaging,
literature, digital media and people culture. Our
marketeers, designers and architects are experienced
in working with major international and local
consultants, agencies and professionals to ensure
the best integrated brand solutions. This proven
brand approach is enhanced by an established
network of local and international specialists.

We have an extensive portfolio of projects in the
retail, financial and real estate sectors. This is
reflected in our recent projects in Russia where we
provide latest brand strategy thinking and design
based on practical resource planning for over 35
clients.

### Clients include

B.A.A. World Duty Free
Burger King
Focus Wickes
Kingfisher Group
Metro Cash & Carry
Nissan, Kuwait
NS Stations, Netherlands
Sainsbury's
Saudi Telecom
Scottish Power
Shell International
Spinneys, U.A.E.
Tchibo
Unilever
Union National Bank, U.A.E.

1  Russian Standard Bank – Russia's largest
   consumer loan bank
2  Econika – Russia's largest fashion footwear retailer
3  Malina – Russia's latest Loyalty Card programme
4  Dixis – Major Russian mobile phone retailer
5  Husasmidjan – Iceland's largest DIY retailer
6  Azbuka Vkusa – Moscow's leading premier
   supermarket group

3

## SCG LONDON
STRATEGIC CONSULTING GROUP

4

6

DIXIS

5

HÚSASMIÐJAN

# АЗБУКА
# ВКУСА

# Springetts

13 Salisbury Place / London W1H 1FJ
T +44 (0)20 7486 7527 / F +44 (0)20 7487 3033
all@springetts.co.uk
www.springetts.co.uk

**Management** Andy Black, Roger Bannister
**Contact** Brendan Thorpe
**Staff** 45 **Membership** Design Business Association

## Company Profile
As one of the UK's top independently owned branding and design consultancies, Springetts has a range of clients from small and local to big and global. Branding can take many forms: a new identity for Barclays sponsorship of the FA Premier League, creation of a new brand for a watch company or a complete overhaul for one of the world's largest football clubs. Springetts has the expertise and experience to offer branding solutions whatever the size and nature of the project.

### See also Packaging Design p. 124

1 British Ecological Society: brand identity and communications
2 Barclays: sponsorship identity
3 Cityspace: brand identity for on-street information service
4 Sekonda: brand creation and communications
5 Manchester United: creation of a new identity system, signage, stationery, tickets, licensing, brand guidelines
6 Bathroom Heaven: brand, retail and print identity

British Ecological Society

1

2

3

## by SEKONDA

5

# bathroom heaven
*love your bathroom*

6

4

# Start Creative Ltd

Medius House / 2 Sheraton Street / Soho /
London W1F 8BH
T +44 (0)20 7269 0101 / F +44 (0)20 7269 0102
jen@startcreative.co.uk
www.startcreative.co.uk

**Management** Mike Curtis and Darren Whittingham
**Contact** Jen McAleer
**Staff** 66 **Founded** 1996 **Memberships** D&AD, DMA,
DBA, IVCA

### Company Profile
Great ideas are rare, yet it is ideas that differentiate
organisations and create value. The best ideas are
also borne of collaborative thinking and working
together.

For over a decade, pursuing this way of working has
allowed us to build lasting relationships, to surprise
and delight our clients and to connect them to their
audiences.

### Clients
Virgin
BBC
Royal Mail
Hertz
uSwitch
Transport for London
Department of Health
COI Communications
Bentley Motors
Up My Street
Visit Britain
Air Partner
Fox Williams
Azzurri

See also New Media Design p. 148 and Interior,
Retail and Event Design p. 190

1   Virgin Atlantic identity
2   Virgin Atlantic 21st Birthday livery
3   Virgin Atlantic Economy, Premium Economy
    and Upper Class photography
4   Virgin Atlantic Flying Club membership cards
5   Flying Club editorial magazine I-Fly
6   Virgin Atlantic credit card
7   Air Partner's JetCard identity and programme
    membership card
8   JetCard launch brochure
9   JetCard microsite
10  Bentley Motors global brand guidelines

1

2

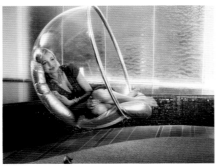

3

4

5

## The Ace of Clubhouses

Would you believe it? Just when you thought our stunning new Heathrow Clubhouse couldn't possibly get any better, it has.

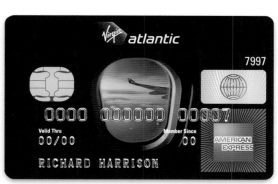

6

## GOOD THINGS COME IN THREES

If one offer is good, and two offers are great, then three offers are positively awe inspiring.

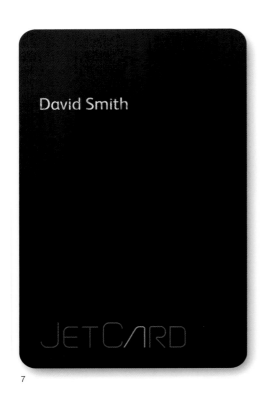

David Smith

JetCard

7

JetCard

8

Slow

Private aviation is the ultimate expression
of personal freedom. With the JetCard,
it's now more accessible than ever.

Fly on a superior fleet of new generation jets,
Bombardier, Cessna, Dassault, Embraer,
Gulfstream and Raytheon.

Breeze in, take off, stretch out, drift away.

Quick

One phone call and we're ready for lift.

9

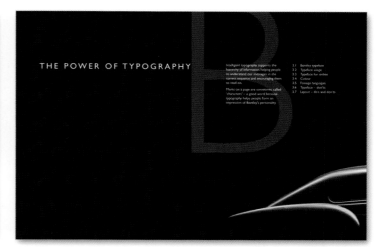

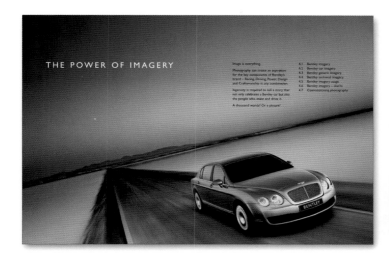

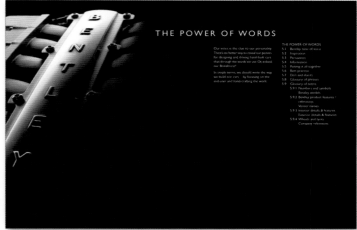

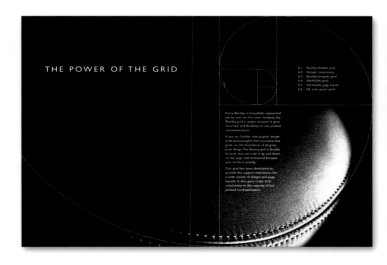

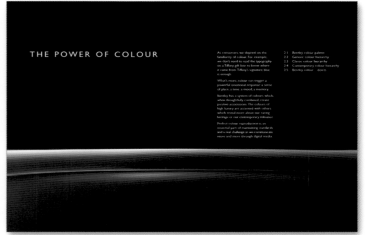

# Studio Output
## Design & art direction

2 Broadway / Lace Market / Nottingham NG1 1PS
T +44 (0)115 950 7116 / F +44 (0)115 950 7924
gemma@studio-output.com
www.studio-output.com

**Management** Rob Coke, Ian Hambleton, Dan Moore
**Contact** Gemma Tabb, Business Development
**Staff** 10 **Founded** 2002

### So, who are we?
We are a design company. We design lots of different things for lots of different people, and we work hard to understand what our clients need to say. Communicating it in the most effective way is what we really do best.

### So, why are we different?
It's not just our work that sets us apart. It's the way we work, with creativity coming from true collaboration, both with our clients and each other. And we encourage direct client contact with the people actually doing the work.

### So, what do we do?
We don't pretend to do everything, but concentrate on what we're good at. We specialise in graphic design, art direction, identity creation, brand development, campaign design, illustration and web styling.

### So, who do we do it for?
Happy clients. That's our only real house style. And whilst the most interesting challenges can come from the most modest projects, we understand that a small list of big hitters can help to inspire confidence. So...

Arts Council England
BBC Radio 1
Channel 4
Coca-Cola
EMI
Ministry of Sound
MTV
Paramount
Schuh
USC

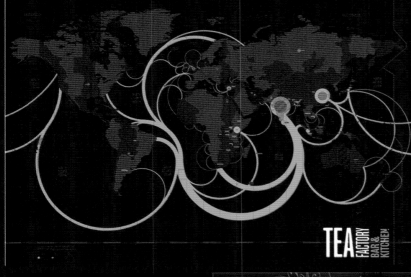

# Tango Design

Newcombe House / 45 Notting Hill Gate /
London W11 3LQ
T +44 (0)20 7569 5700 / F +44 (0)20 7569 5656
info@tangodesign.com
www.tangodesign.com

**Contacts** Dana Robertson, Alice Moore

**Company Profile**
Tango is an award-winning brand communications
agency that expresses brands in a fresh and
contemporary way. We are a cutting-edge design
store that understands the real value of creativity
and knows the strategic importance of design to our
clients. Through our work with a number of leading
clients in the international youth market, Tango has
accumulated a wealth of knowledge in all areas of
brand communication and retail brand presence
strategy. We like to think that our designs combine
the wisdom of experience with the energy of youth.

**Clients Include**
Nike
Gatorade
Dockers
Sony
Vodafone
Levis
Amnesty International
Harvey Nichols
Rainforest Foundation

1 Rainforest Foundation
2 Pout
3 Nike Shox Rival
4 Gatorade
5 Nike Tuned 1
6 Nike Original

1.

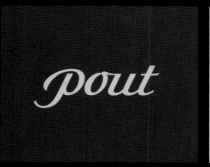

2.

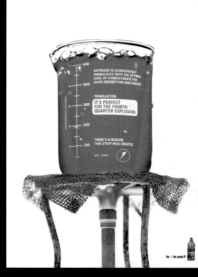

3.

4.

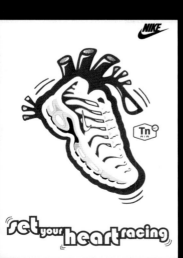

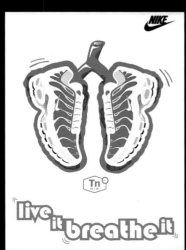

# TWO:design
## Creative Direction & Design

Studio 37 / Hampstead House / 176 Finchley Road / London NW3 6BT
T +44 (0)20 8275 8594
studio@twodesign.net
www.twodesign.net

**Management** Graham Peake MA MCSD
**Contact** Zoe Davies
**Staff** 5 **Founded** 1997 **Memberships** Chartered Society of Designers, British Design Initiative

### Profile
TWO:design is an independent creative consultancy which offers Creative Direction, Design and Brand Consultancy to a growing, diverse international client base.

With extensive project experience in brand creation, evolution and extension, we offer a boutique service which is strategy and prediction driven for all corporate, technology, entertainment, retail and fashion clients.

We are comfortable working at board level with international brands and clients, as part of a rostered team of suppliers or as a 'hot shop' with larger global advertising agencies. We look forward, not back.

### Clients
*Technology*
Agile Media/British Telecommunications PLC. Elanders Infomedia AB. The Worldwide Bluetooth Congress/Informa PLC.

*Entertainment*
Sony BMG Entertainment: Columbia, Epic, Ovum, Sony Urban, Sony International, Work Records. Columbia Tristar Pictures. Warner Music UK. EMI Music UK. RuffHouse/Trimedia LLC. FatWreckChords SF. MTV UK & Ireland. Sony Playstation™/Atari/ Reflections Games.

*Performance Clothing & Fashion*
Kangol. Karrimor. Merrill/Wolverine footwear. Sells Goalkeeper Products. Valsport. Spencer Hart Tailors (Savile Row, NY & LA).

*Product Design/Manufacturing & Architecture*
D4 Display UK & North America. Michael Dowd Architectural Associates. JLA Architects London.

*Retail, Interiors, Exhibitions & POS*
JafflePie (UK). Liberty's Menswear (London). Merrill/Wolverine footwear (UK shows). Sells Goalkeeper Products (Global). Sony BMG Entertainment (Global). Spencer Hart (Savile Row).

### Press
The studio has featured in numerous design articles and publications, notably: 'Cool Type Two' (Northern Light/USA), 'The Science of Music Icons' (Brazen/Singapore), 'plus 81 magazine' (D.D.Wave/Japan), 'Design Week' and 'Creative Review' (Centaur/UK).

e.magazine 'Shift' commented: 'The work of this small London studio is spot on.' TWO:design received a BPI award in 1998 for artist work with Sony/ Columbia Records.

# Über

Royds Mills / Windsor Street / Sheffield S4 7WB
T +44 (0)114 278 7100
info@uberagency.com
www.uberagency.com

**Management** Richard Benjamin, Pamela Jayne
Broadberry, Greg Clark **Contact** Jonathan Jesson
**Staff** 17

**Company Profile**
See www.uberagency.com

**Our Client Partners Include**
Activision
B Braun
Consort Homes
Department for Education and Skills
DFS
Empire Interactive
Gamestracker
Interface
Mental Health Foundation
Midway
Morphy Richards
React Snowboards
Sony Computer Entertainment
Take2
Top Up TV
Vector
Yorkshire Air Ambulance
Zoo Digital Publishing

1   Corporate Brochure, Vector OEM
2   Corporate Identity, Cutting Edge Technology
3   'Head Gear' Brand Identity, Morphy Richards
4   Corporate Identity, Top Up TV
5   Audio Brand Identity, Morphy Richards
6   'Head Gear' Packaging Design, Morphy Richards
7   Event Campaign, Cultural Industries Quarter
    Agency
8   'Half Price' Outdoor Campaign, DFS
9   'Sale' Outdoor Campaign, DFS
10  'Tony Hawk's Underground 2' In-Store POS
    Campaign, Activision
11  Various Snowboard Designs, React Snowboards

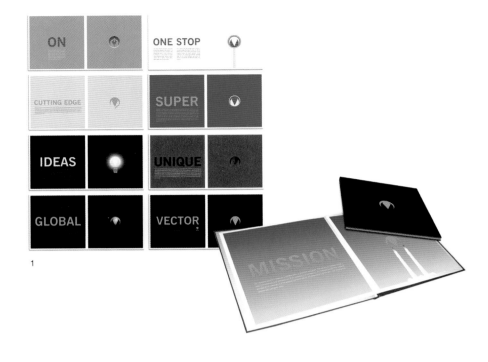

1

6

10

2

4

5

3

7

8

9

11

# Un.titled
## Design & Art Direction

Un.titled / 21 Wellington Street / Leicester LE1 6HH
T +44 (0)116 247 1111 / F +44 (0)116 247 0909
darren@un.titled.co.uk
www.un.titled.co.uk

**Management** Giles Marshall, Darren Jessop,
John Kariolis, Matt Culpin **Contact** Darren Jessop
**Staff** 25 **Founded** 1997

**Company Profile**
Formed in 1997, we are a full service creative agency.
We enjoy long-term collaborative and creatively
charged relationships with some of the world's largest
and most influential brands. Our work is defined by
our obsession with strong ideas, our belief in the
power of great design, and our dedication to the
success of the brands with whom we work.

**Expertise**
Digital Design
Moving Image
Brand and Corporate Identity
Print Design and Publishing
Photography
Art Direction

**Clients**
Accessorize
Ben Sherman
Boxfresh
Clarks
Clarks Originals
Dazed and Confused
Evisu Shoos
John Smedley
Keenpac
Kickers
Lacoste
Lee Cooper
Next
Nike
Pointer
Puma
SML
Speedo
Visual Thinking
Wembley National Stadium

1-2    Branding for 'ONE' range, John Smedley
3-4    Moving image presentation for 2006, Puma
5      Branding, Keenpac
6      Branding, Taste Inc
7-8    Product collection for 2007, SML
9-10   Brochure for the watch and jewellery market,
       Keenpac
11     Website, Kickers
12     Website, Lee Cooper
13     Initial concept designs for web and brand
       project, Clarks Originals
14-15  Microsite for Considered range, Nike
16     Branding, Pointer

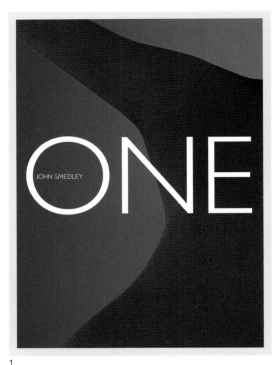

2

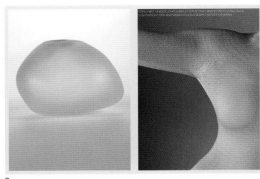

1

3

4

5

keenpac

**Taste inc.**

6

7

8

9 – 10

13

11

14

15

12

16

pointer

# Z3
## www.designbyz3.com

Loft 2 / Broughton Works / 27 George Street /
Birmingham B3 1QG
T +44 (0)121 233 2545 / F +44 (0)121 233 2544
info@z3ltd.com
www.designbyz3.com

**Management** Richard Hunt, Scott Raybould
**Contacts** Richard Hunt, Scott Raybould
**Staff** 6 **Founded** 1992

### What drives us
Creating desire through innovation, communicating
through design. We provide integrated highly visible
campaigns in all mediums. We produce inspiring,
engaging communication solutions that work.
Our experience spans the corporate and public
sectors, the arts, music industry, packaging, and
leisure industry. View our creative output on-line
www.designbyz3.com

### Clients
New Balance
Vicon Motion Systems
Geospatial Vision
Sony Music Entertainment
Warner Music
Wolverhampton & Dudley Brewery
Simple (Accantia Health & Beauty Ltd)
Glenn Howells Architects
Birmingham City Council
Sofa Brands International
Marketing Birmingham
NEC Group (Symphony Hall)
University of Central England
Associated Architects
Ikon Gallery
Natratec.com
Logica CMG
Umberto Giannini Hair Cosmetics
Boots plc
Museum of Modern Art Oxford
Pitt Rivers Museum Oxford
University of Warwick
Iguana Exhibitions Group
Big Life Records
Gatecrasher
Birmingham Contemporary Music Group
DanceEast
Public Arts Commissions Agency
University of York
York City Art Gallery

**New Balance**
In-store point of sale

**Solarstone Destinations Volume 1**
www.deepbluerecords.co.uk

**Umberto Giannini Hair Cosmetics**
www.umbertogiannini.com

**Slinky Trans-Atlantik**
CD Packaging

**New Balance 100th Centenary**
Press Pack and CDrom

**Ikon Gallery**
Exhibition Book

**MOMA Oxford**
Exhibition Literature

**Deep Blue Recordings**
CD Packaging

   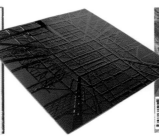 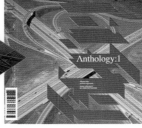

**Packaging Design**

# Blackburn's Ltd
## Brand Design

1A Clarkson Row / Camden Town / London NW1 7RA
T +44 (0)20 7383 4360 / F +44 (0)20 7383 5739
emily@blackburnsdesign.com
www.blackburnsdesign.com

**Management** John Blackburn, Executive Creative
Director, Belinda Duggan, Creative Director
**Contacts** Emily R Miller, Marketing Director
**Staff** 8 **Founded** 1966

**Company Profile**
Blackburn's Ltd, recently relocated to Camden Town,
has over 30 years of experience in brand packaging
design – handling a broad international client base
from large multi-nationals to small independent
companies.

Our belief is that the strongest brand identities are
those built on a 'Big Idea'. Ideas drive creativity:
they define a brand's personality and are a key to
commercial success. Decorative graphics are not
enough: to have any real impact, packaging must
be distinctive, emotive, campaignable and ownable.

Our expertise includes NPD, brand reappraisal,
structural design, name generation, logo creation
and supporting promotional material. We offer a
bespoke service to suit any marketing strategy.

Blackburn's has won over 100 major awards around
the world for both creativity (D&AD, Clio, Epica) and
for design effectiveness (DBA, Marketing and Drinks
International).

VOLUMISE SHAMPO ADDICTED CANDY ADDICTED CHERRY CHEW

CONDITION SHAMPO CANDY ADDICTED MANGO TANGO

COLOUR ENHANCE SHAMP ADDICTED CANDY ADDICTED PINK GRAPEFRUTTI TUTTI

THE CONSULTANCY
Lucinda Ellery
★ ★ ★ ★ ★
For Exceptional Hair
SHAMPOO

THE CONSULTANCY
Lucinda Ellery
★ ★ ★ ★ ★
For Exceptional Hair
CONDITIONER

THE CONSULTANCY
Lucinda Ellery
★ ★ ★ ★ ★
For Exceptional Hair
BALM

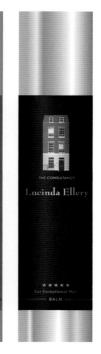

# dare!
## brand identity & packaging

3 East Causeway Close / Leeds LS16 8LN /
West Yorkshire
T +44 (0)113 281 7080 / F +44 (0)113 281 7088
dare.smt@virgin.net
www.dareonline.co.uk

**Contacts** Debbie Seal, Simon Tame
**Founded** 1998

Specialising in the alcoholic beverages sector since
1998, dare! work with both small and large producers
and importers worldwide, refreshing existing
packaging and creating new brands for the global
market.

Our success is not measured by awards alone, but,
more importantly, by the loyalty of our clients and
packaging that performs in a highly competitive
market sector.

wine sellers

# Enterprise IG
## The Global Brand Agency

11-33 St John Street / London EC1M 4PJ
T +44 (0)20 7559 7000 / F +44 (0)20 7559 7001
info@enterpriseig.com
www.enterpriseig.co.uk

**Contact** John Mathers, UK CEO
**Founded** 1976

Enterprise IG is one of the world's leading
international brand agencies that has the resource of
nearly 600 people, covering 22 offices in 20 countries.

Enterprise IG believes that great companies and their
brands are built on a Compelling Truth™. A truth so
powerful it is transformational – building preference
and differentiation with consumers, customers and
employees. At Enterprise IG we partner with our
clients to find the Compelling Truth™ that underpins
their company, product or service brands.

We provide first-class Strategy, Design and
Engagement advice to major multinational and local
blue-chip clients. Our extensive range of skills and
experience, engaging both internal and external
audiences, ensures that the Compelling Truth™ is
delivered at all touch points – from identity, brand
architecture and communications through packaging,
product design, POS, brand language, retail
manifestation, brand experience, brand environment,
live events and interactive media.

See also Branding and Graphic Design p. 36,
New Media Design p. 142 and Interior, Retail and
Event Design p. 176

# Identica

Newcombe House / 45 Notting Hill Gate /
London W11 3LQ
T +44 (0)20 7569 5600 / F +44 (0)20 7569 5656
info@identica.com
www.identica.co.uk

**Contacts** Ron Cregan, Pierre Boyre

**Company Profile**
At Identica we understand the commercial value of
a unique idea. Ideas are our raw material, and with
them we create powerful, distinctive and compelling
communication as well as strategic direction for some
of the world's most interesting businesses.

We've worked on some of the world's largest
brands...and some of the smallest start-ups. Our
confidence comes from knowing that we have years
of experience coupled with some of the freshest
creative talent and up to the minute knowledge of
some of the world's newest technologies.

We work in all aspects of branding and packaging
design across many sectors: food and drink, sport,
fashion, retail, technology, telecoms, health & beauty,
pharmaceutical, and many others.

We like to think that we provide the best of both
worlds: the most outstanding creative work as well as
the kind of joined-up thinking that you would expect
from a large integrated agency.

If you believe your business could benefit from the
in-put of creative, engaging, eclectic and challenging
minds, we'd like to hear from you.

**Clients Include**
Diageo
Ocean Spray
Campbells
Tesco
Roust Inc
Planters
Unilever
Chivas Regal
Penhaligon's
Pernod Ricard

1   Russian Standard Vodka
2   Johnnie Walker
3   Captain Morgan Tattoo
4   Flagman Vodka
5   Smirnov Vodka
6   Kitchen & Pantry
7   Russian Standard
8   Johnnie Walker
9   GB Wines, Russia
10  Kitchen & Pantry
11  Ocean Spray
12  Campbell's Selection Soups
13  Urban Garden Honey Co.

1.

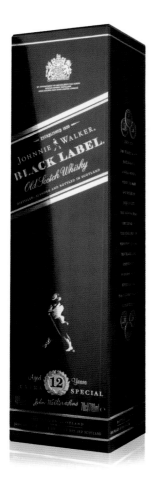

2.

3.

4.

5.

6.

7.

8.

9.

10.

11.

12.

13.

# jones knowles ritchie

128 Albert Street / London NW1 7NE / Camden
T +44 (0)20 7428 8000 / F +44 (0)20 7428 8080
info@jkr.co.uk
www.jkr.co.uk

**Founded** 1990

**Winning in a 1 second world**
There are 25,000 items in the average supermarket,
yet only 55 go into the average shopping trolley.
And only 75 minutes to choose them in.

Impulse purchasing drives your brands' success.

Fight commoditisation with distinctive and engaging
design! Design that puts the brand first, not the
consumer, so it can't be 'adapted' by your friends
at the supermarkets.

Nice theory, but does it work in practice? Send
a blank email to samcarrington@jkr.co.uk and we'll
send you some data, so you can judge for yourself.

**Principal Clients**
Britvic
Heinz
Kraft
Masterfoods
Molton Brown
RHM
Unilever

BY APPOINTMENT TO HM THE QUEEN
MANUFACTURER OF SUGAR
BRITISH SUGAR PLC PETERBOROUGH
silver
spoon
sugar
CASTER
PERFECT FOR LIGHTER BAKING
BY APPOINTMENT TO HM THE QUEEN
MANUFACTURER OF SUGAR
BRITISH SUGAR PLC PETERBOROUGH
silver
spoon
sugar
JAM SUGAR
WITH ADDED PECTIN

# Osborne Pike

Bath Brewery / Toll Bridge Road / Bath BA1 7DE
T +44 (0)1225 851 551 / F +44 (0)1225 858 228
steve@osbornepike.co.uk
www.osbornepike.co.uk

**Management** Steve Osborne, David Pike, David Rivett
**Contacts** Steve Osborne, Sharon Brunt
**Staff** 5 **Founded** 2002

We create packaging that communicates with people, recognised in an instant as an old friend or a new temptation. Ideally both.

**We work with...**
Almaza
Batchelors
Dormen's
Douwe Egberts
Duyvis
Fresh Daisy
Heineken
Hildon
LU
Pickwick
Sanex

# pi global

1 Colville Mews / Lonsdale Road / London W11 2AR
T +44 (0)20 7908 0808 / F +44 (0)20 7908 0809
hello@piglobal.com
www.piglobal.com

**Management** Don Williams, CEO
**Contacts** Vanessa Lumby, Client Services Director;
Pia Badziong, Marketing and Research Manager
**Staff** 60 **Founded** 1984

## Company Profile

Founded in 1984, pi global are an independent
branding, visual brand id application and packaging
design consultancy. We operate out of our Notting Hill
offices in London with international, multi-disciplinary
teams.

pi global's fundamental passion is 'iconistic® brand
id' – our branding methodology and core philosophy,
the focus of which is the optimisation of our clients'
investment in communication and the long term
health and growth of the brands we work on – our
aim is always to provide vastly improved saliency
and facilitation of stretch and growth for our clients'
brands.

We specialise in all areas of FMCG and Healthcare
branding, id application and packaging design.
From billion dollar Global brands to 'local jewels' –
we have created, strengthened and protected many
of the world's most recognised, long lasting and
commercially successful brand identities.

As well as brand strategy, planning, design,
stewardship and implementation, pi global offer
our clients a wide range of disciplines through our
specialist divisions: brand ideation and innovation
through pid8 – consumer and retail observation and
analysis as well as 'real-world' research consultancy
through picu – structural design, engineering,
production and prototyping through pi3.

Based on an understanding of the role of branding
and how it relates to pack design, communication
and consumers – our single-minded philosophy
provides real 'cut through' and delivers clear, concise,
consistent and unambiguous brand messages: we
understand how to optimise brand triggering AND
category/range/product communication on packaging
and PDP to fully leverage in-store commmunication.

## Services Include

Brand Strategy; Brand Naming; Brand and
Technical Futures; iconistic® Brand Id; Visual
Brand Architecture; Visual Brand Audit; New Brand
Development (nbd); New Product Development
(npd); Pack Graphic Design; Pack structural
Design; Structural Packaging Innovation; Prototype
Development; Management of Tooling, Development
and Sourcing; Consumer/retail observation and
analysis; Research Consultancy; Production
Consultancy; Technical Management; Brand
Stewardship; Marcomms.

## Clients Include

Procter & Gamble; Twinings; Bayer Healthcare;
Masterfoods Europe; Akzo Nobel; Carlsberg; Arla;
Reckitt Benckiser.

**See also Branding and Graphic Design p. 72**

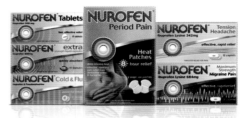

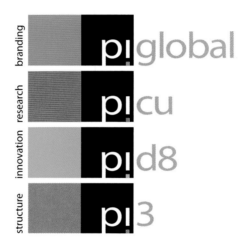

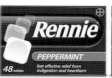
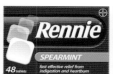

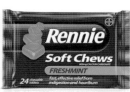

# Pure Equator
## Packaging & Brand

The Old School House / The Heritage Centre /
High Pavement / The Lace Market /
Nottingham NG1 1HN

Australian Office / Suite 7.05 6A Glen Street /
Milsons Point / Sydney NSW 2061 / Australia

T +44 (0)115 947 6444 / M +44 (0)7989 322 304 /
F +44 (0)115 950 4948
david.rogers@pure-equator.com
www.pure-equator.com

**Management** David Rogers, Sue Allsopp
**Contact** David Rogers
**Staff** 30 **Founded** 1999

Pure Equator is the small (award winning) design
consultancy with the big personality with offices in
Nottingham (UK) and Sydney (Australia). We specialise
in all elements of the marketing mix, to get the
products on and off the shelf; from branding and
packaging, through to P.O.S. Our company culture,
coupled with our innovative yet commercial design,
ensures that we consistently delight our clients by
offering extra ordinary value for money. Our clients
range from Super Brands to small independent food
producers.

London International Awards 2005
Package Design - gold

AWARD WINNING

label.m
CLEANSE + REPAIR SHAMPOO

label.m
REPAIRING CONDITIONER

Mobius Awards 2005
Certificate for Design Excellence

PURE
EQUATOR
DESIGN CONSULTANTS

rapid·white

tooth whitening system
méthode de blanchiment des dents

2 4 6 8 10

Up to **6** shades lighter in **14** days
6 nuances plus claires en 14 jours

45 applications
45 traitements de blanchiments

Fast acting **3 step** system
Système d'action rapide de 3 étapes

Clinically proven
Médicalement avéré

TONI&GUY
defined cream wax

MEN ONLY

100ml

**London International Awards 2005**
**Package Design – finalist**

From those that matter

"Working with Pure has been a revolutionary experience. Pure have been dedicated and committed to going that extra mile to deliver something extra special for TONI&GUY. From innovative packaging ideas, to design creation, and working with pace to deliver tight deadlines, Pure have delivered consistently and beyond expectation!"

– Jacqui Pearson, Brand Manager, Toni & Guy

"I worked with David for 3 years while at Wella and was not only impressed with his creativity, but thrilled to find an agency with solid experience of the beauty business. 5 years on and I have continued my relationship with Pure on the basis that it is hard to find a 'great' agency, with a 'can-do, will-do' attitude, that I can trust to deliver time and time again! Highly recommended!"

– Nikki McReynolds, Brand Manager, Amplex

"The new design of our Just Brazils packaging is the best I have seen in the confectionery market for a number of years and I am delighted with the results."

– Tracey Wilson, Marketing Director, Fox's Confectionery

PURE
EQUATOR
DESIGN CONSULTANTS

# Reach

Hope Chapel / Battle Lane / Chew Magna /
Bristol BS40 8PS
T +44 (0)1275 332 296 / F +44 (0)1275 331 399
caroline@reachdesign.co.uk
www.reachdesign.co.uk

**Management** Richard Evans, Caroline Hagen,
Mark Rylands **Contact** Caroline Hagen
**Staff** 13 **Founded** 1998
**Membership** Design Business Association

Established in 1998, Reach is a strategic packaging
design consultancy based in Bristol. With London
expertise and relaxed South West surroundings, we
adopt a friendly, thoughtful, collaborative approach to
packaging design that continues to result in engaging
and effective design solutions for many familiar
household brands.

We always ensure that through watertight strategy
we are in tune with your business and consumer,
applying the same enthusiasm to every project
regardless of its size. This has helped us create and
build brands that really sustain their significance in
the marketplace, as well as forge relationships with
brand owners that are truly long lasting.

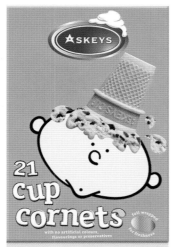
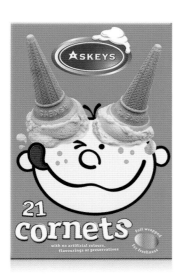

re&ch

# Springetts

13 Salisbury Place / London W1H 1FJ
T +44 (0)20 7486 7527 / F +44 (0)20 7487 3033
all@springetts.co.uk
www.springetts.co.uk

**Management** Andy Black, Roger Bannister
**Contact** Brendan Thorpe
**Staff** 45 **Membership** Design Business Association

## Company Profile
As one of the UK's top independently owned branding and design consultancies, Springetts has a range of clients from small and local to big and global. Our expertise in packaging design is demonstrated in the range and longevity of many of our client relationships. Our honesty and integrity allow us to build strong working partnerships where clients deal directly with strategically literate designers, not account handlers.

**See also Branding and Graphic Design p. 84**

1 Twinings: packaging design and communication
2 Georgia Pacific: brand identity and packaging
3 Maxell: packaging identity
4 Campbell's: brand and packaging redesign

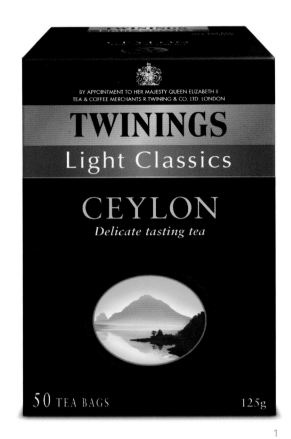

1

2

3

4

# Springetts

## Brand Design Consultants

FOR FURTHER INFORMATION
CONTACT ANDY BLACK
TEL: 020 7486 7527
www.springetts.co.uk

# Stocks Taylor Benson Ltd
## Graphic Design
## Consultancy

The Forge / Unit 10 Desford Road / Narborough
Wood Business Park / Enderby LE19 4XT /
Leicestershire
T +44 (0)116 238 7833 / F +44 (0)116 239 3407
trevor@stbdesign.co.uk
www.stbdesign.co.uk

**Management** Glenn Taylor, John Benson
**Contact** Trevor Flannery
**Staff** 28 **Founded** 1988
**Membership** Design Business Association

**Company Profile**
Stocks Taylor Benson is a creative graphic design
consultancy that produces design solutions for
packaging, literature and point of sale.

We are very straightforward and practical.

We love what we do, we enjoy working together with
our clients and we are pround of our results.

Whatever the project, we realise graphic design is
about solving problems and the only reason we are
working with our clients is for our solutions to directly,
or indirectly, generate a greater income for them.

Our aim, at all times, is to provide our clients with
excellent design, excellent value and, above all
excellent service.

**Clients**
Alliance & Leicester
Antalis
Blacks
Freespirit
Herbalife
Interflora
Julian Graves
Kitchen Craft
Millets
Morrisons
Next
Nivea
Slazenger
Vax

graphic
design
consultancy

for...

# excellent design

**"** We produce designs that are creative, innovative, unique and commercial **"**

# excellent value

**"** We produce the **very best,** commercial graphic design solutions money can buy **"**

and, above all

# excellent service

**"** We are customer focused at all times offering a level of **professional service unsurpassed by our peers "**

# Two by Two
## Design Consultants

348 Goswell Road / London EC1V 7LQ
T +44 (0)20 7278 1122 / F +44 (0)20 7278 1155
zebra@twobytwo.co.uk
www.twobytwo.co.uk

**Management** Salvatore Cicero, Ashwin Shaw
**Contact** Nikki Wollheim
**Staff** 7 **Founded** 1995 **Membership** BDA

**Company Profile**
Small is beautiful and particularly so in our world.
There are 7 valued team members at Two by Two,
working to an ethos and in an environment that
encourages creativity, resourcefulness and self
development.

Both partners are actively involved in the planning,
management and art direction of all projects. We
offer a dedicated team and personal service for each
client, combining a blend of fresh creative ideas,
with extensive experience of the processes involved
in translating visual ideas into practical workable
solutions.

The success of our particular approach to design
is demonstrated by the long-lasting and close
relationships that we build with our clients,
culminating in a product of which we are all proud.

Two by Two believe in the power of creativity and
the craft of implementation. And it works.

Originality breeds content.

**Clients Include**
Biotherm
Cottages to Castles
Cosmedicate
Elemis
Goldman Sachs
In Harmony
Intermix
L'Oréal Group
Magnelli Coffee
Nicole Farhi
The Royal Mint
Sainsbury's
Saki Bar and Food Emporium
Teenage Cancer Trust
Triumph
Verco
The Wine Society

**See also Interior, Retail and Event Design p. 194**

1   Nicole Farhi Fragrance packaging for men
    and women

# Vibrandt
## Global Brand Design Agency

Old Brewery / Russell Street / Berkshire /
Windsor SL4 1HQ
T +44 (0)1753 624 242
lovebrands@vibrandt.co.uk
www.vibrandt.co.uk

**Management**
Ray Armes – Chairman
Jayne Lilly – Managing Director

**Vibrandt Thinking…**
We know that there's more to a brand's life than just packaging!

Like people, brands should know who they are and what they are about, have ideals and dreams for the future.

We will help you develop brand ideas and philosophies that can become the lifeblood of all brand activity, not just create great design for packs…

*Vibrandt is an award winning global creative agency. Specialists in brand development and design; working from brand strategy, positioning and name generation, to brand identity & packaging design.*

**UK/South Africa/New York (from 2007)**

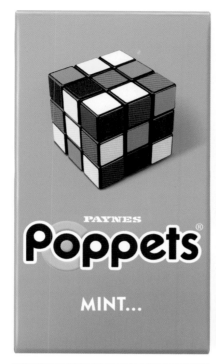

PAYNES
**Poppets**®

MINT...

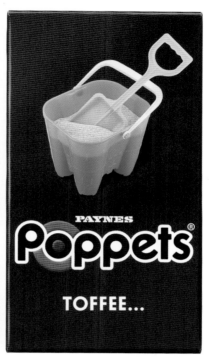

PAYNES
**Poppets**®

TOFFEE...

PAYNES
**Poppets**®

RAISIN...

PAYNES
**Poppets**®

ORANGE...

**Vibrandt** growing brands

# Ziggurat Brands

8-14 Vine Hill / Clerkenwell / London EC1R 5DX
T +44 (0)20 7969 7777 / F +44 (0)20 7969 7788
ziggurat@zigguratbrands.com
www.zigguratbrands.com

**Management** Adrian Collins, Allison Miguel,
Kellie Chapple **Contact** Adrian Collins
**Staff** 15 **Founded** 1984 **Memberships** DBA, D&AD,
Marketing Society

Ziggurat…we believe in creating a smile in the mind

At Ziggurat we believe in the power of design to
deliver profitable brand growth.

Be it naming, creating a new brand identity,
packaging design or corporate identity we are
committed to delivering what we term Meaningful
Change; change with reason, change with relevance,
change with results.

We believe that great design communicates
emotionally and as consumers increasingly use
brands as beacons round which to navigate their
lives, the brand identity has a bigger role to play
as a prime mover in helping form and develop
the emotional bond with its consumer than simply
standing out on the shelf; it's the silent persuader.

In the area of packaging design for instance, we
believe that the pack is unique in the marketing mix
in having access to consumers away from the point
of sale. It has access to the unguarded sub-conscious
mind. A real relationship can be built with them over
time if there's something to engage with. Trialists
become advocates and then advocates become
lovers; not as romantic a notion as that may seem.

We've a clutch of effectiveness awards that proves
that award-winning creative work can deliver serious
competitive advantage.

*Jonathan Crisp*™

MATURE CHEDDAR
& RED ONION.
*Crisps for snobs*

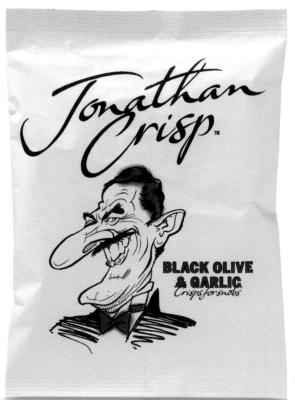

*Jonathan Crisp*™

BLACK OLIVE
& GARLIC.
*Crisps for snobs*

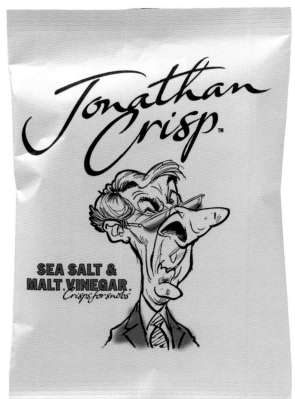

*Jonathan Crisp*™

SEA SALT &
MALT VINEGAR.
*Crisps for snobs*

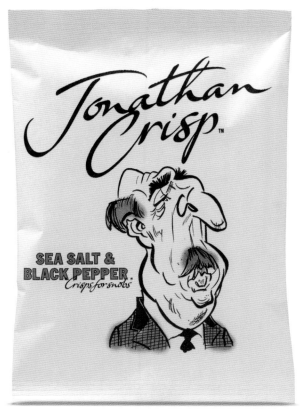

*Jonathan Crisp*™

SEA SALT &
BLACK PEPPER.
*Crisps for snobs*

# Clusta Ltd

31-41 Bromley Street / Birmingham B9 4AN
T +44 (0)121 604 0004 / F +44 (0)121 604 3344
hello@clusta.com
www.clusta.com

**Management** Matthew Clugston, Russell Townsend
**Contact** Andrew Bowyer
**Staff** 14 **Founded** 1997

Clusta is home to a collective of the finest designers
working with some of the world's biggest brands.

Since our inception, we've embraced the digital media
and built a name for consistently innovative design.

**Our Services**
Web Design
Flash Design
Database, E-Comm and CMS Solutions
Video & Post Production
Animation
3D Visualisation
Riveting Conversation
Branding
Graphic Design
Illustration

**Our Clients**
Helix
Carphone Warehouse
Amnesty International
Channel 4
Orange
Pacha Group
Defected Records
Glue London
RPM Ltd
Agency.com
Tibbatts Associates

**See also Branding and Graphic Design p. 32 and
our sister company ClustaSpace in New Media
Design p. 138**

01_Deluka 'I'll Wait' Video Promo
Filmed in HD, extensive green screening and post-production
work was employed to keep the band's gritty style
02_Orange Studio Sting
Bespoke character designs composited in video editing
software and utilised to illustrate the studio's versatile
structure whilst retaining a credible look and feel

01

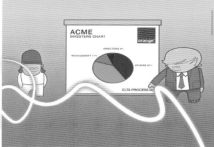

02

**Clusta**

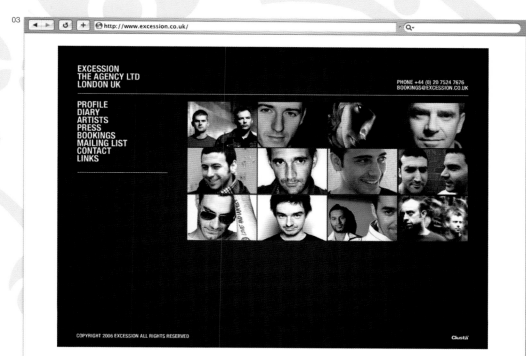

## CaseStudies
### Yo!Sushi and iPod

Yo! Sushi have enjoyed massive success since their first restaurant opened in 1997 . . . . but staying cool needs cool friends.

Back then diners were amazed by Sushi on conveyor belts, robotic drinks trolleys and airline style service buttons. But what seemed state of the art then isn't going to seduce new customers today and brands like Yo! Sushi need to constantly evolve to stay ahead of the rest.

Blend were given the ultimate brief; deliver a technological partner who's super cool, has Japanese connotations and is able to move quickly i.e. cut through the red tape of bureaucracy.

back™ next™

03_Excession The Agency Ltd: www.excession.co.uk
Content managed website

04_Pacha London: www.pachalondon.com
Fully content managed website

05_Happi Madison: www.happimadison.com
Content managed e-commerce website

06_Carbon Music Store: www.carbonmusic.com
Content managed e-commerce website

07_Seymour Harris Architecture: www.seymourharris.com
Content managed website

08_Blend: www.blenduk.com
Content managed website with bespoke 'matching' database

# ClustaSpace
## 3D Visualisation and Interior Architecture

31-41 Bromley Street / Birmingham B9 4AN
T +44 (0)121 604 0004 / F +44 (0)121 604 3344
hello@clustaspace.com
www.clustaspace.com

**Management** Steve Ellis, Russell Townsend,
Iain Johnson, Ben Dawson, Matthew Clugston
**Contact** Russell Townsend

ClustaSpace Ltd is a young and fresh visualisation, animation & architectural services company. Created by a group of like minded individuals drawn from creative and architectural backgrounds, we have over 30 years combined experience within the industry. Our collective skills give us the edge across a host of digital media and we are regarded as specialists in our field.

Amongst our services, we provide state of the art 3D visualisation and animation, including visually stunning photorealistic stills, moving image and architectural walkthroughs. All are ideal for effectively promoting and showcasing new developments, products or venues, with our fresh creativity enabling maximum impact.

We work to provide our clients with the highest quality visual assets for their projects including; interactive and multimedia presentations, printed material and product rendering as well as supplying physical models.

**Services**
3D Visualisation & Animation
Interior Architecture
Photography
Physical Model Making

**See our sister company Clusta Ltd in Branding and Graphic Design p. 32 and New Media Design p. 136**

006

007

001 | Product Rendering - Wine labels and bottles
Premier Estates

002 | Detailed Kitchen Rendering - Frame from animation
The Point, IE Developments Ltd

003 | Detailed Bathroom Rendering - Frame from animation
The Point, IE Developments Ltd

004 | Contextual External Rendering
Regency Mews, Cheltenham, Dodd homes Ltd

005 | Detailed Lounge Apartment Rendering
Frame from animation
The Point, IE Developments Ltd

006 | Detailed Live/ Work Apartment Rendering
Hylton Street, Holloway Foo/ InTheDetail

007 | Detailed Commercial Office Rendering
Windmill Street, Stephenson Bell Ltd

"ClustaSpace are positive and imaginative.
They take the trouble to understand why you
want something not just what you want, and it
helps that they're talented too!"

Steve Evans, MD and Founder, Rekk limited

**ClustaSpace**

# Creative Edge
## Design and Web Consultants

Riverside House / Heron Way / Newham /
Truro TR1 2XN / Cornwall
T +44 (0)1872 260 023 / F +44 (0)1872 264 110
mail@creativeedge.co.uk
www.creativeedge.co.uk

**Management** David Rickett, Melinda Rickett
**Contact** Melinda Rickett
**Staff** 10 **Founded** 1992 **Memberships** The Chartered
Society of Designers, DBA

### Company Profile
We are a Westcountry based award-winning creative
design and web consultancy, with over 25 years
experience in design solutions for local, national and
international clients.

### Clients
Actnow Broadband Cornwall
British Telecom
Carrs Audi
Chester City Council
Cornwall County Council
Duchy Originals
Furniss Foods
Highgrove
Kettle Produce
Midas Construction
National Maritime Museum Cornwall
Plunkett Foundation
Royal Cornwall Museum
Soil Association
The National Trust
Truro School
University of Exeter
University of Plymouth
Visit Cornwall
Westcountry Investments

1   South West Penninsula
2   Friends of Restronguet Point
3   Artchart Architects
4   Kernow Kampers
5   Rural Cornwall & Isles of Scilly Partnership
6   Actnow Broadband Cornwall
7   St Michael's Hotel
8   Innovate Centre for Creative Industries
9   Royal Cornwall Museum
10  Jetscene
11  Cornwall Association of Tourist Attractions
12  Visit Cornwall

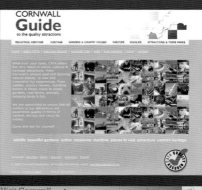
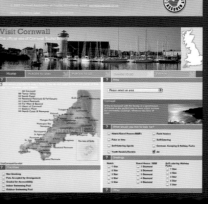

# creativeedge.co.uk

identity
brand development
design for print
web design
packaging
exhibitions
interiors
signage
advertising

# Enterprise IG
## The Global Brand Agency

11-33 St John Street / London EC1M 4PJ
T +44 (0)20 7559 7000 / F +44 (0)20 7559 7001
info@enterpriseig.com
www.enterpriseig.co.uk

**Contact** John Mathers, UK CEO
**Founded** 1976

Enterprise IG is one of the world's leading
international brand agencies that has the resource of
nearly 600 people, covering 22 offices in 20 countries.

Enterprise IG believes that great companies and their
brands are built on a Compelling Truth™. A truth so
powerful it is transformational – building preference
and differentiation with consumers, customers and
employees. At Enterprise IG we partner with our
clients to find the Compelling Truth™ that underpins
their company, product or service brands.

We provide first-class Strategy, Design and
Engagement advice to major multinational and local
blue-chip clients. Our extensive range of skills and
experience, engaging both internal and external
audiences, ensures that the Compelling Truth™ is
delivered at all touch points – from identity, brand
architecture and communications through packaging,
product design, POS, brand language, retail
manifestation, brand experience, brand environment,
live events and interactive media.

**See also Branding and Graphic Design p. 36,
Packaging Design p. 108 and Interior, Retail and
Event Design p. 176**

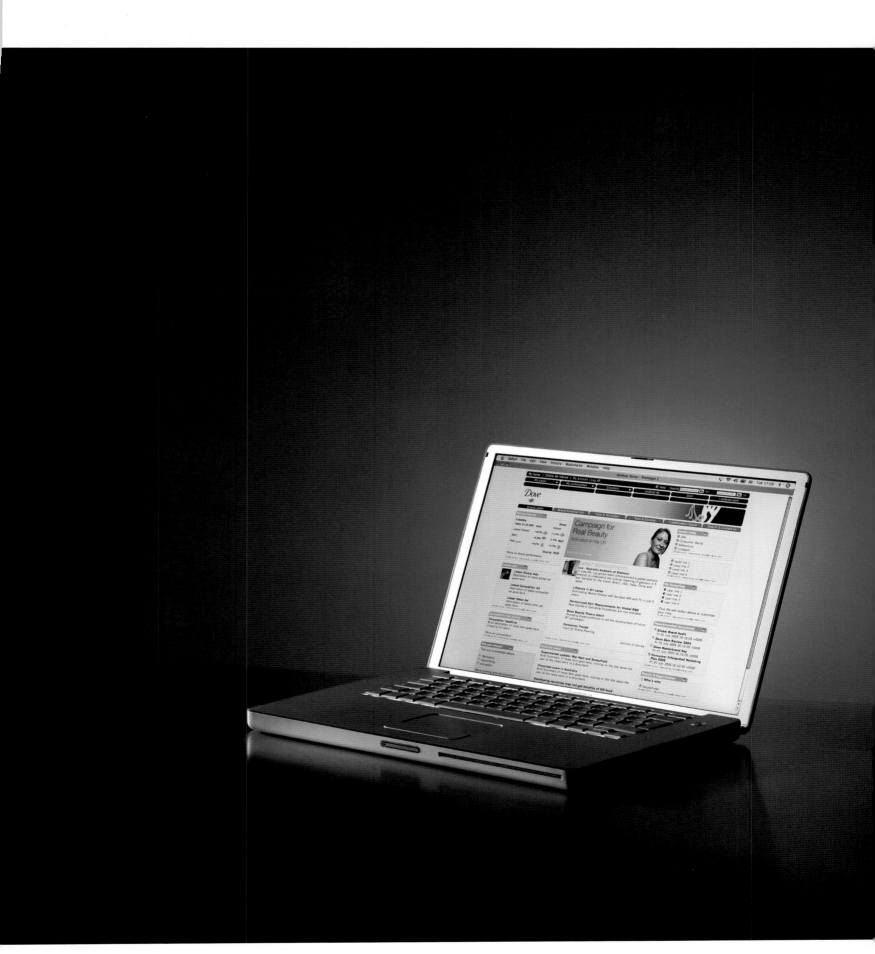

# Lloyd Northover

2 Goodge Street / London W1T 2QA
T +44 (0)20 7420 4850 / F +44 (0)20 7420 4858
trudi.osborne@lloydnorthover.com
www.lloydnorthover.com

**Contacts** Trudi Osborne, Jim Bodoh, Matt Silcock
**Founded** 1975 **Memberships** DBA, D&AD, CBI,
CSD, IOD, RSA, IIID, BDI, The Design Council,
The Marketing Society, Sign Design Society

## We build vivid brands and engaging online experiences

We are a team of inventive, down-to-earth people
devoted to creating memorable and engaging
brand experiences. We help to make this happen
through your communications online and in print,
through your people, and within your environments.

Our digital consultants work hard to get under
the skin of your business, the needs of the people
you want to engage with, and the market context in
which you operate. Through our technical expertise,
robust analysis, challenging creative standards
and disciplined project management, we create
interactive strategies and experiences that bring
your brand to life.

With our unique approach, we strike just the right
balance between analysis and inspiration to deliver
outstanding results.

### Our interactive services include:
Research and analysis
Strategic e-business and online brand consultancy
Web services
Content and application development
Channel and brand management
e-marketing

If you like what you see, get in touch to find out what
we've done for others and, more importantly, what we
can do for you.

### See also Branding and Graphic Design p. 66

1  becauseyoucan website
2  Star website
3  Training and Development Agency for Schools
   website
4  National Savings and Investments website –
   winner of DBA Design Effectiveness Award 2005

1

3

2

4

**Lloyd Northover**

# Pod1
## Shiny, Happy People!

223 Westbourne Studios / 242 Acklam Road /
London W10 5JJ
T +44 (0)870 246 2066 / F +44 (0)870 246 2065
contact@pod1.com
www.pod1.com

**Management** Fadi Shuman, Marc Caudron
**Contacts** Fadi Shuman, Marc Caudron
**Staff** 35 **Founded** 2001
**Memberships** British Interactive Marketing
Association, British Design Initiative, Internet
Advertising Bureau, UK Web Design Association

### Company Profile
Pod1 is a specialist web design, development
and online marketing agency.

Here at Pod1 we are passionate about building
high impact websites that deliver business results
for our clients with a clear focus on usability and
accessibility. It is our aim to create websites and
online marketing campaigns that inspire, inform
and effectively communicate the right message
to the target audience.

A London based, independent agency, we have
been providing expert web design, development
and online marketing services for the last five years.

Established in 2001, the company has continued
to go from strength to strength while building an
impressive client portfolio along the way.

Ranked in the top 100 UK design companies
by Design Week magazine (June 2006), we supply
the very best in creative and technical expertise.

### Clients
Shell
Hiscox
Chrysalis
Kenwood
Hi-Tec Sports
Tesco
United Nations
Lastminute.com
Yahoo
Hachette Fillipacchi
FremantleMedia
Thomson
Paramount Hotels
Matches
Mr & Mrs Smith
Autotrader
BBC
Pepsi

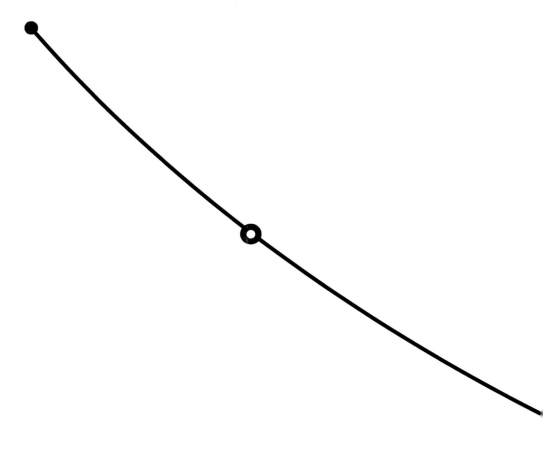

## Our **Work & Clients**

**Paramount**
www.paramount-hotels.co.uk

**KangaROOS**
www.kangaroos.co.uk

**Hi-Tec**
www.hi-tec.com

**Hiscox**
www.hiscox.co.uk

**Mr. & Mrs. Smith**
www.mrandmrssmith.com

**Links of London**
www.linksoflondon.com

# Start Creative Ltd

Medius House / 2 Sheraton Street / Soho /
London W1F 8BH
T +44 (0)20 7269 0101 / F +44 (0)20 7269 0102
jen@startcreative.co.uk
www.startcreative.co.uk

**Management** Mike Curtis and Darren Whittingham
**Contact** Jen McAleer
**Staff** 66 **Founded** 1996 **Memberships** D&AD, DMA,
DBA, IVCA

### Company Profile
Great ideas are rare, yet it is ideas that differentiate
organisations and create value. The best ideas are
also borne of collaborative thinking and working
together.

For over a decade, pursuing this way of working has
allowed us to build lasting relationships, to surprise
and delight our clients and to connect them to their
audiences.

### Clients
Virgin
BBC
Royal Mail
Hertz
uSwitch
Transport for London
Department of Health
COI Communications
Bentley Motors
Up My Street
Visit Britain
Air Partner
Fox Williams
Azzurri
Scrawl Collective

**See also Branding and Graphic Design p. 86
and Interior, Retail and Event Design p. 190**

1 BBC brand website
2 Virgin Atlantic Online Check In animation
3 Virgin Galactic launch broadcast video
4 Hertz Car's integrated campaign
5 Scrawl Collective website

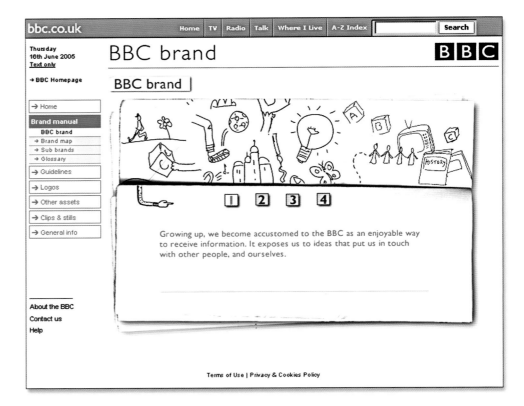

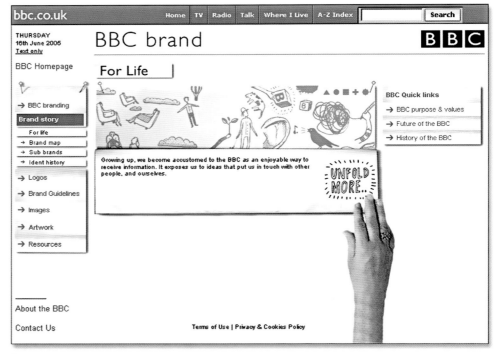

1

2

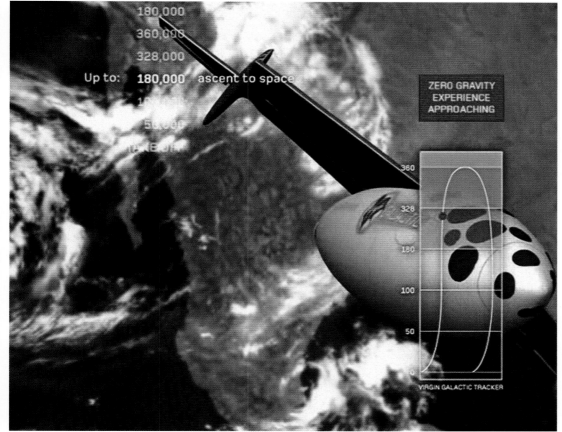

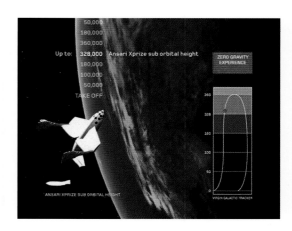

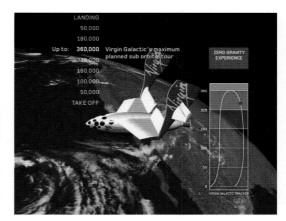

3

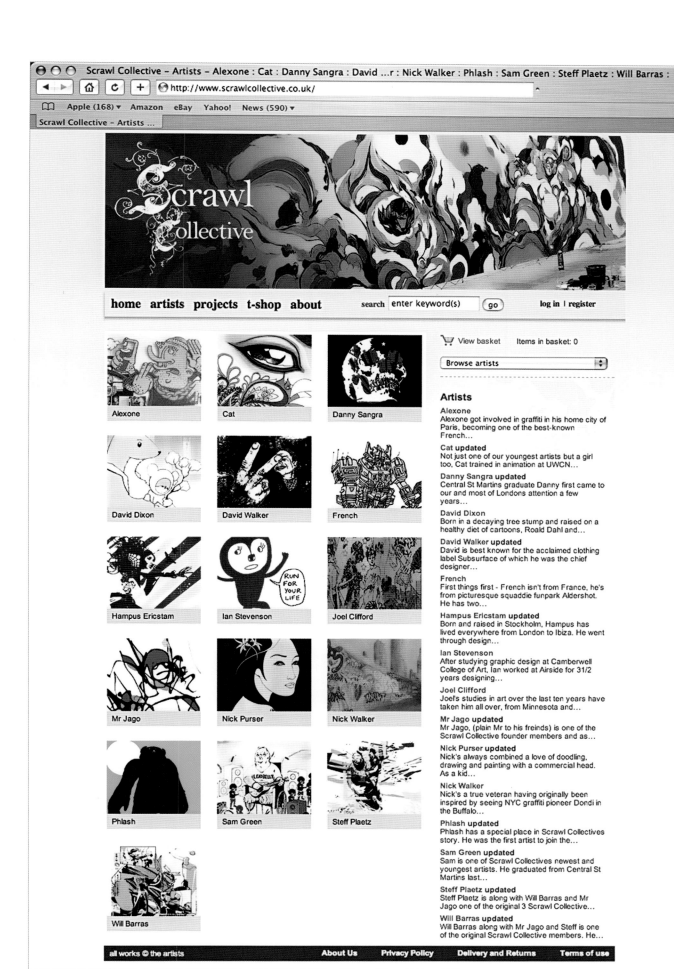

# unit9.
## Interactive Agency

The Lux Building / 2-4 Hoxton Square /
London N1 6NU
T +44 (0)207 613 3330
hello@unit9.com
www.unit9.com

**Contacts** Piero Frescobaldi, Tom Sacchi
**Staff** 18 **Founded** 1996 **Memberships** D&AD,
The One Club, BIMA, IVCA, IAB, COI Roster

**Company Profile**
Creativity is at the centre of our business, it is backed
by strategy, technical expertise and strong project
management. unit9 staff come from all over the world
and many different disciplines. This diversity is the
engine of our creativity.

"Our work aims to engage people at an emotional
level. At our very best we create remarkable online
experiences that can change how people feel."
Piero Frescobaldi, Creative Director.

**Awards**
Recently declared one of Campaign Magazine's
'Online's Finest', unit9's work has won awards for
creativity and effectiveness, including Cannes Cyber
Lions, Design Week Awards, D&AD Awards, The
One Show, London International Advertising Awards,
Revolution, NMA, Bima.

**Clients/Brands**
Adobe
Aida Capital
American Airlines
BBC
DiscoverCard
Eidos
Evian
Framestore CFC
Gorgeous Productions
Goodby Silverstein & Partners
HP
IBM
Lufthansa
MasterCard
McCann Erickson
Nestle'
NHS Barts & The London
Ogilvy
Panasonic
Prudential
RKCR/YR
Sony SCEE
Sony Vaio Japan
The Sunday Times
Tourism Ireland
Victoria & Albert Museum
Virgin Mobile
Vodafone
Warner Music
Wieden+Kennedy
Yahoo!

unit9.com/kitchen

Pasta is the only non-digital thing we do.

### national eco
for tyo-id japan

### discovercard - send an elf
for goodby silverstein & partners san francisco

**152**

### mastercard - keep it hidden for christmas
for mccann erickson london

### v&a - modernism
for the victoria & albert museum

### virgin mobile v-festival
for rainey kelly campbell rolfe

### honda - grrr
for wieden + kennedy london

# UsTwo
## Creative Design Studio

7-10 Batemans Row / London EC2A 3HH
T +44 (0)20 7613 0433
sinx@ustwo.co.uk
www.ustwo.co.uk

**Management** Matt Miller, John Sinclair
**Contact** John Sinclair
**Staff** 9 **Founded** 2005 **Membership** D&AD

### Company Profile
UsTwo is a creative design consultancy formed in response to the burgeoning possibilities of interaction design. We conceive, design and build innovative solutions for websites, mobile devices, the television and automative industries. We create memorable brands and entertaining content. Our approach is driven by a desire to create innovative, aesthetic, experiences which please the senses.

### Our Clients Include
Sony Ericsson
Sony
Ford
The London Institute

1 Deltalighthome.co.uk – Website
   www.deltalighthome.co.uk
   A website launched to sell lighting with a subtle mix of function and design, for the home.
2 Universal Leonardo – Website
   www.universalleonardo.org
   The largest and most comprehensive on-line resource of Leonardo da Vinci's work.
3 Ferguson Freeview Box – Interface
   Design of the on-screen interface for Dixon's own brand Freeview Box.
4 Ford Motor Company – Ford Geneva HMI
   Design and production of the 'Human Machine Interface' and Digital Dashboard for the Ford Visos concept car, exhibited at the 2005 Geneva Motorshow.
   – Received 'in book' status at D&AD 2005 and awarded Commended at Design Week Awards 2005
5 Ford Motor Company – Ford Visos HMI
   Design and production of digital dashboard and onboard computer to reflect the customer focused technology of the Ford Visos.
   – Received a Silver nomination at D&AD 2004

1

2

3

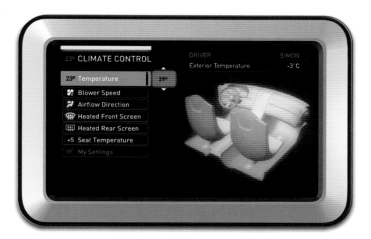

4

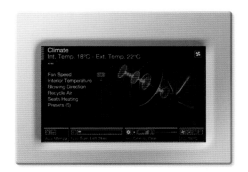

5

# View

The Penthouse, Long Island House /
1-4 Warple Way / London W3 0RG
T +44 (0)20 8740 9751
bguly@view.uk.com
www.view.uk.com

**Management** Eddie Blitz, Bernard Guly, Mark Smith,
Charles Smith, Ann Longley **Contact** Bernard Guly
**Staff** 30 **Founded** 1992

### Company Profile

We plead guilty to being obsessive. The client comes
first and last ...and everywhere in between. Set them
a project and our team – strategic, creative and
production – delight in thinking their way inside the
box. It's our tried and tested formula for producing
those imaginative digital communications and brand
solutions that delight our clients.

Which is why View is recognised by blue chip
companies in many sectors as the strategic brand
and digital communications agency of choice.

Broadband is everywhere. The array of increasingly
mobile media options is evolving rapidly. Many
switched-on FTSE companies have grasped that
this is a great opportunity. For the first time they have
the chance to keep in constant touch with all their
stakeholders – and to lead the debate on key issues
in their sector.

We have had a decade and a half's experience in
looking to the future. Our teams love to work long-
term with clients, applying our expertise in digital
marketing, editorial strategy, brand reputation and
corporate social responsibility.

Think 'V2B' – the strategic brand and digital
communications agency of choice.

### Clients

BlackBerry
BP
British Heart Foundation
Dell
Diageo
GlaxoSmithKline
International Power
Network Rail
OMD
Rio Tinto
Rolls-Royce
Sterling Energy
Urenco
Value Retail

# You may not have heard of us, but the company we keep speaks volumes.

v:ew

The strategic brand and digital communications agency

Interior, Retail and Event Design

# BDP Design

16 Brewhouse Yard / Clerkenwell / London EC1V 4LJ
T +44 (0)20 7812 8000 / F +44 (0)20 7812 8399
m-cook@bdp.co.uk
www.bdpdesign.co.uk

**Management** Martin Cook **Contact** Martin Cook
**Staff** 46 **Founded** 1972

BDP Design is a multi-discipline design group with a wide range of skills and expertise across both public and private sectors. Our experience spans retail, leisure, education, workplace, healthcare and transport design.

Our key strength lies in the integration of a wide range of creative services and solutions from a single source. Numerous leading brands are represented by many of our clients, with whom we have formed lasting relationships in both the UK and throughout Europe.

We believe in bringing the best skills and experience together to produce customer-focussed solutions.

1-6 'The Place', the Royal Society of Ulster
　　Architects, Belfast
2-3 Roche, Welwyn Garden City
4-5 BSkyB, New Horizons Court, London

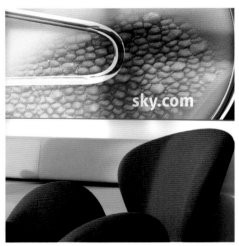

# Briggs Hillier Design

Alma House / Wibtoft / Lutterworth /
Leicestershire LE17 5BE
T +44 (0)1455 221 919 / F +44 (0)1455 221 019
design@briggshillier.com
www.briggshillier.com

**Management** Adrian Briggs, Jenny Hillier
**Contacts** Jenny Hillier, Paaru Chauhan-Pancholi
**Founded** 2000 **Membership** DBA

## Company Profile
As brand and retail specialists, Briggs Hillier Design
offer a full range of services tailored around creating
successful retail design solutions.

Our strength is understanding our clients business,
'getting inside' their brand, and realising the
aspirations of their target market by delivering design
that works.

When it comes to our approach, our aim is to
continually exceed the expectations of our clients
and their customers, by realising the full potential
of any brand or retailer.

## Services
Brand Strategy
Retail Interiors
Shop in Shop
Communications
Instore Graphics
Packaging
Project Management

All photos: Schuh, New Store Concept, Bluewater

**brand**&**retail** specialists

briggs hillier design

# CampbellRigg

8-9 Apollo Studios Charlton Kings Road /
London NW5 2SB
T +44 (0)20 7284 1515 / F +44 (0)20 7267 4112
design@campbellrigg.com
www.campbellrigg.com

**Management** Campbell Rigg, Dorota Czernuszewicz
**Contact** Dorota Czernuszewicz
**Founded** 1987

### Company Profile
CampbellRigg is an independent design agency
renowned for its international work in the field of retail
interiors and retail communications. The company
provides strategic and creative design solutions to
some of Europe's most successful businesses.

We have significant experience in adding economic
value to our clients' businesses by designing store
environments, developing retail formats, graphic
communication suites and producing innovative
merchandising solutions to improve their retail outlets.

Utilising our belief in 'total design' – a creative activity
involving imagination, intuition, financial common
sense and deliberate choice, our international team
of Strategic Planners, Interior and Graphic Designers
and Architects partner these businesses with the
vision of obtaining the best returns on capital
employed.

### Clients
Manor AG – Switzerland
Adler Modemärkte GmbH (Metro Group) – Germany
Kaufhof AG (Metro Group) – Germany
OBI GmbH (Tengelmann) – Germany
Interspar – Austria
Kesko OY – Finland
ICA OY – Sweden
Musgrave Supervalu Centra – Ireland
Argos Stores Ltd – United Kingdom
Safeway Stores plc – United Kingdom
Woolworths plc – United Kingdom
Comet Group plc – United Kingdom
Dixons Stores plc – United Kingdom
Harvey Nichols plc – United Kingdom
Harrods Ltd – United Kingdom
Arcadia plc – United Kingdom
Contessa – Courtald Textiles – United Kingdom
Chelsea Girl – Concept Man – United Kingdom
Unilever plc – United Kingdom
Whitbread plc – United Kingdom
Cadbury Schweppes plc – United Kingdom
McDonalds – United Kingdom
Abbey National plc – United Kingdom
Barclays Bank plc – United Kingdom

1-4 Harrods, UK
5     Argos, UK
6     Centra, Ireland
7     Safeway, UK
8     Adler, Germany
9     Blockbuster, UK
10    Woolworths, UK
11    Kesko Citymarket, Finland
12    Comet, UK
13    Haspa, Germany

1

2

Cooking

Dishwashers

3

4

14.09.06 LONDON
The 9th annual **RETAIL INTERIORS AWARDS**

Department Store Interior of the Year
campbell rigg design
for Harrods

finalist

bellriac

5

6

9

12

campb

7

8

10

11

13

ellrigg

# Checkland Kindleysides Ltd

Charnwood Edge / Cossington / Leicester LE7 4UZ /
Leicestershire
T +44 (0)116 2644 700 / F +44 (0)116 2644 701
info@checkind.com
www.checkind.com

**Management** Jeff Kindleysides; Claire Callaway,
Managing Director
**Staff** 85 **Founded** 1979

## Company Profile
We are an independent design group and we believe
our culture is unique. We're collaborative, inventive
and resourceful and we've 26 years of experience
and knowledge of consumer facing design. We work
in partnership with both national and international
brands across a wide range of market sectors.

## Expertise
Identity
Communications
Environment
Merchandising
Packaging
Exhibitions
Consultancy

## Clients
Audi, Bentley Motors, Boots, California Academy of
Sciences, Comet, Design Council, Dunhill, George at
ASDA (Walmart), Hammersons (Bullring Development),
Henri-Lloyd, HSBC, KFC, Kohler Mira, Ladybird, Levi
Strauss, Marks & Spencer, Mobiltel, Ozwald Boateng,
Roland, Sony Computer Entertainment, Sony
Electronics, Thorntons, Timberland Boot Company,
Truworths, Virgin Megastores, WGSN.

## Awards
Future Marketing Awards 2006
Levi's Revolution – Best Use of Retail

Chain Store Age Awards 2005
Timberland Boot Company Store – International
Category

POPAI Europe Awards 2005
Sony PSP Sampling – Leisure, Electronics,
Hi-Fi & Video Category

Marketing Design Awards 2005
Boots No7 – Sales Promotion & Point of Purchase
Category

**See also Branding and Graphic Design p. 30**

1 Mobiltel Retail Concept, Bulgaria
2 Sony PSP Consumer Experience Unitary
3 Boots No7 Retail Merchandising
4 Levi's 'Revolution' Pan European Retail Concept

1

2

3

4

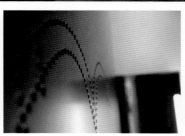

# Corsie Naysmith Design

Unit 4.06 Clerkenwell Workshops
27-31 Clerkenwell Close / London EC1 0AU
T +44 (0)20 7375 0768
k.corsie@corsie-naysmith.co.uk
s.naysmith@corsie-naysmith.co.uk
www.corsienaysmith.com

**Management** Ken Corsie, Stuart Naysmith

### Company Profile
Corsie Naysmith Design is a London based, award-winning, international retail design consultancy that boasts amongst its clients some of the most prestigious new generation manufacturers, retailers and brands.

We are committed to a vision of creativity and methodology, working in partnership with our clients to achieve highly creative, commercially successful design solutions.

We are a multicultural chain of skilled and knowledgable people who make the marketplace innovative, exciting and stimulating to the consumer by creating a story around the product. We call this process Global Merchandising.

In our retail design process there are four entry points that help you to build a story around the product:

Product development
Product assortment
Retail environment
Brand communication

Our teams of designers, visual merchandisers, graphic artists, brand and marketing consultants will guide you through the design process, helping you take control of the vision for your brand.

### Some of our current clients include
adidas
B&Q
Channel Islands Co-operative
Calmia
Diageo
Li & Fung Group
Kingfisher
Salomon
Smirnoff
Spyker Cars
Thomas Cook
Wolsey

A full client list is available on request

corsie**naysmith**design

global

1 | 2 | 3 | 4 | 5

**1**
Harrods
Designer
Collections

Through our **global merchandising** process we were able to quickly identify the commercial aims of the brief whilst creating a minimal contemporary space within the world's most famous department store.

**2**
Calmia

Our **global merchandising** team helped this wellbeing and holistic lifestyle brand to organise their product collections, clarify their offer to the consumer and create a retail environment that established the future vision for the brand.

**3-4**
Salomon

Through our **global merchandising** approach we were able to work with all aspects of the brand to include product placement, visual merchandising, retail environment and brand identity creating the first 3D representation of the worlds leading action and outdoor sports brand.

**5**
Harrods
Accessories
Collections

With our **global merchandising** vision we identified the future merchandising possibilities for all aspects of the luxury branded offers, both in terms of products and sales densities to deliver the commercial aims that the client had anticipated.

# merchandising

**1** To confer sense and meaning on an otherwise inanimate object through the brand

**2** The ability to create and evoke the product story to challenge, engage and seduce the consumer

**3** To provide innovation, added value and a consumer experience in the global presentation of your product

**Spyker**

Through our **global merchandising** process we provided innovation, added value and consumer experience in the global presentation of one of the world's most exclusive luxury automotive brands.

Corsie Naysmith Design is an Associated Member of the Global Merchandising Network

# Dalziel and Pow

5-8 Hardwick Street / London EC1R 4RG
T +44 (0)20 7837 7117 / F +44 (0)20 7837 7137
info@dalziel-pow.co.uk
www.dalziel-pow.co.uk

**Management** David Dalziel, Rosalyn Scott,
Jackie Ware, Keith Ware and Alastair Kean
**Contacts** David Dalziel, David Wright
**Staff** 55 **Founded** 1983

## Company Profile
A leading player in the UK and international market
of design services, specifically for retailers and their
brands, we strongly believe in the role of Retail
Design to connect 'shoppers' with brands, bringing
both financial and emotional benefits. From fashion to
technology and from value to premium brands, 3000
projects in over 60 countries in 23 years is testament
to our continued success in our chosen discipline.

Utilising our unique blend of 2D and 3D skills we
develop design solutions that exceed our clients'
targets and expectations.

## Expertise
Retail Design and Interiors
Brand Development and Name Generation
In-store Graphics and Point of Sale
Packaging
Art Direction
Web Design and In-store Multimedia

## Clients
Arnotts
Blacks
Duffer of St George
Evans
Gap
Hugo Boss
Illum
JDSports
Jones Bootmaker
Kotva
Lee
Millets
Motivi
NCR Design Centre
Nokia
Plaisio
Primark
River Island
Speedo
Stylo
T-Mobile
Toyota
Villandry
World Duty Free
Wrangler

## Recent Awards
Retail Interiors Awards 2006
Best Out of Town Store – Blacks, Romford

Retail Week Awards 2006
Best New Store Design – River Island, Bluewater

Retail Interiors Awards 2005
Best Small Shop – Speedo, Covent Garden

Dalziel and Pow are a founding member of
ALL-AROUND-DESIGN, a European association
of independent design consultants.

DESIGN

# FOR RETAIL

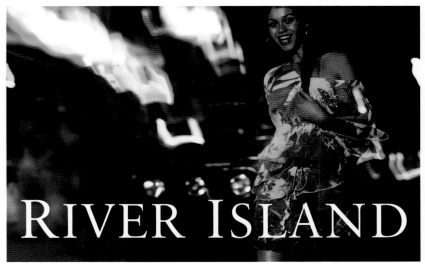

RIVER ISLAND

DALZIEL + POW

# Enigma Creative Solutions Ltd
## Sharper by Design

119-120 High Street / Eton SL4 6AN / Berkshire
T +44 (0)1753 496 470 / F +44 (0)1753 496 482
dominic.softly@enigmaCS.com
www.enigmaCS.com

**Management** Richard Pryer, Alan Surman,
Dominic Softly **Contact** Dominic Softly
**Staff** 21 **Founded** 1987

Multiple award-winning.

Reliable.

Adaptable.

Intelligent.

Creative.

From initial brief to your ROI, we deliver on
exhibitions, events, video production, new media,
websites & print – and all points between.

Enigma look at the big picture and the telling detail.
Result? End-to-end solutions. Globally. Think of us
as a Creative Intelligence Agency. (The other CIA).

"Everything should be made as simple as possible,
but not simpler." Albert Einstein

### Selected Clients
Adobe
Airbus
British Airways
British Telecom
Compaq
DTI
Fiat
Indesit
Intel
Mobil
National Lottery
Orange
Philips
QinetiQ
Royal Mail
Shell
Siemens
BSkyB
Sony UK
Sun
Royal Navy
Toshiba
Ubisoft
Union Bank of Switzerland
Virgin Atlantic

### See also Branding and Graphic Design p. 34

1  Party & Live Entertainment
2  Trade Show Environment
3  Branding & Design
4  Interior
5  New Product Launch, Exhibition & POS
6  Theatre & Live Action
7  Product Launch & Content
8  Immersive Showroom
9  Video
10 Print & New Media
11 Interactive Museum Experience

8

5

7

9

## Individual Attention

10

11

# Enterprise IG
## The Global Brand Agency

11-33 St John Street / London EC1M 4PJ
T +44 (0)20 7559 7000 / F +44 (0)20 7559 7001
info@enterpriseig.com
www.enterpriseig.co.uk

**Contact** John Mathers, UK CEO
**Founded** 1976

Enterprise IG is one of the world's leading international brand agencies that has the resource of nearly 600 people, covering 22 offices in 20 countries.

Enterprise IG believes that great companies and their brands are built on a Compelling Truth™. A truth so powerful it is transformational – building preference and differentiation with consumers, customers and employees. At Enterprise IG we partner with our clients to find the Compelling Truth™ that underpins their company, product or service brands.

We provide first-class Strategy, Design and Engagement advice to major multinational and local blue-chip clients. Our extensive range of skills and experience, engaging both internal and external audiences, ensures that the Compelling Truth™ is delivered at all touch points – from identity, brand architecture and communications through packaging, product design, POS, brand language, retail manifestation, brand experience, brand environment, live events and interactive media.

**See also Branding and Graphic Design p. 36, Packaging Design p. 108 and New Media Design p. 142**

# Fitch

121-141 Westbourne terrace / London W2 6JR
T +44 (0)20 7479 0900 / F +44 (0)20 7479 0600
david.balko@fitch.com
www.fitch.com

**Management** Rodney Fitch (wordwide), Lucy Unger,
Tim Greenhlagh (London) **Contact** David Balko
**Staff** 80 **Founded** 1972 **Memberships** D&AD, ISTD,
CSD, DBA

## Company Profile

Fitch is one of the world's best known and most
influential design agencies. Fitch has a unique focus
on retailing in all its forms, and is expert in designing
consumer brands and retail environments.

Fitch has over 450 associates in 18 different studios
across 11 countries working across time zones to
retail the goods, services and personalities of our
clients all over the world.

## Redefining Retail

The world of retail is changing dramatically and is
becoming more competitive. People are taking control
and require different ways to engage with brands,
they seek brands, products, services and
environments that connect with them emotionally and
enhance their lives beyond functionality to deliver
experiences that match their aspirations.

Fitch's strategy of 'Redefining Retail' recognizes these
changes as we enable brands to retail their stories to
consumers in ways that are relevant and engaging
through the channel and experience of their choice.

## Clients Include

Vodafone
Nokia
BAT
Carhartt
Amsterdam Schiphol Airport
2006 Doha Asian Games
Yum brands
DSG
Goodyear Dunlop
Lego
Harrods
Hyundai
Russian Post
Microsoft
Central Food halls

See also Branding and Graphic Design p. 40

01

02

03

04

05

LEGO
**01** Brand store design
DUNLOP
**02** Autosport exhibition
CENTRAL FOOD HALL
**03** New identity and premium consumer food experience

VODAFONE
**04-05** Global standard store design
CARHARTT
**06** Trade show launch of work wear brand

# JHP Design

Unit 2 / 6 Erskine Road / London NW3 3AJ
T +44 (0)20 7722 3932 / F +44 (0)20 7586 7048
austin.m@jhp-design.co.uk
www.jhp-design.com

**Management** Steve Collis, Raj Wilkinson
**Contact** Austin McGinley
**Staff** 22 **Founded** 1979

### Company Profile
At JHP we conceive commercial experiences that
enable our clients to 'sell' more of whatever it is they
make, buy or acquire.

Our skills have been developed at the commercial
front line – the only true interface of customer,
product and brand – the retail environment.

There are as many sectors in retail as there are
commodities and aspirations in life and over the last
three decades JHP has grappled with most of them.

What we haven't helped to sell probably hasn't
been invented yet and whether our clients make
their own product, buy and sell someone else's,
or develop centres and rent space to those that do,
we never allow ourselves to be constrained by the
methodologies of any particular creative discipline.

### Services
Architecture
Retail environmental design
Art direction

### Clients
Selfridges
Hyundai
Barclays
Dunhill
O2
British Gas
Heineken
Cadbury
BAA
Free Duty Hong Kong
British Airways
Boots
Waitrose
ASDA
Hypercity
Pizza Express
Timberland
ESPRIT
Accessorize
RNLI
Hammerson

1  Maxi Markt, Salzburg
2  Salta, Barcelona
3  Accessorize, London
4  Wrangler, Manchester
5  Giorgio Armani, Global

2

3

4

5

# Kinnersley Kent design

5 Fitzroy Square / London W1T 5HH
T +44 (0)20 7691 3131 / F +44 (0)20 7691 3141
audra@kkd.co.uk
www.kkd.co.uk

**Management** Mr Mick Kent, Mr Glenn Kinnersley,
Mr Paul McElroy **Contact** Audra Francis
**Staff** 20 **Founded** 1990 **Memberships** British Design
Innovation, Institute of Directors

## Company Profile
Kinnersley Kent design specialise in retail design
for Department Stores, Fashion and Food Retailers,
Restaurants, Supermarkets and Variety Stores.
Successful projects are created for clients using a
process driven by a passion for design, commercial
awareness, knowledge and a professional culture.

## Expertise
Retail Design Specialists
Interior Architecture
Graphics & Point of Sale
Brand & Corporate Identity
Packaging
Web & Multimedia

## Clients
Albert Roux
Bateel
Big W
Booths
Boots
Compass Group
Dorothy Perkins
Fortnum & Mason
House of Fraser
Marks & Spencer
Massarella Catering Group
Menarys
Mercedes-Benz
Morgan
Palmer Sport
Roja Dove
Texas Homecare
Tishman Speyer Properties
WH Good

01

01 > 04
House of Fraser, Norwich,
Dundrum & Birmingham

05
Fortnum & Mason, flagship
London and Japan

06
Bateel, flagship London
and Middle East

02

03

04

05

06

# Land Design Studio Ltd

46 High Park Road / Kew TW9 4BH
T +44 (0)20 8332 6699 / F +44 (0)20 8332 6095
info@landdesignstudio.co.uk
www.landdesignstudio.co.uk

**Management** Peter Higgins, James Dibble,
Shirley Walker **Contact** Peter Higgins
**Staff** 10 **Founded** 1992 **Membership** RIBA

### Company Profile

Having developed our core skills within the museum
domain, we have continued to acknowledge a gradual
shift that has provided the opportunity to apply our
design methodology to more commercial activities.
This shift is simply a function of user needs where
the leisure marketplace has encouraged convergence;
museums, zoos, themed experiences, world expos
even shopping are simply contrasted and compared
by the ever-discerning consumer.

Our overriding mantra remains the same; we need to
understand the fundamentals of architectural space,
narrative content, and the appropriate use of
communication media, all of which helps create a
sustainable visitor destination.

A strong architectural background has enabled us to
gain the confidence of a number of highly reputable
architects, resulting in well-considered and integrated
solutions. We have found that both architect and
interpretive designer must acknowledge each other's
function and develop genuine mutual respect.
Apparently obscure issues may impact on each of
them.

In respect of communication media our greatest
strength has been in developing intuitive digital
installations. At the National Waterfront Museum
Swansea we were able to use the technology to
'unlock glass cases', provide access to archive
material and help visitors to understand their sense
of place – through landscape mapping. In contrast,
for the UK Pavilion at the Japan Expo'05 we created
very simple sensory interfaces that described a wide
range of fascinating initiatives that had enabled UK
scientists to develop their technologies, by
referencing the natural world. This project surpassed
the clients expectations by attracting 3m visitors,
achieved extensive media coverage and has
subsequently received five international awards
including the Art Directors Club (New York) Gold
Award for interactive media.

### Clients

Anschutz Entertainment Group
Ars Electronica (AT)
BBC
Centre of the Cell
Expo Zaragoza 2008 (ESP)
Foreign & Commonwealth Office (UK)
Imperial War Museum (London)
Louis Vuitton (Paris / Taipei)
Ministry of Tourism & Antiquities Jordan
Miraikan – National Museum of Emerging Science
& Innovation, Tokyo
National Museums & Galleries Wales
National Railway Museum
Natural History Museum (London)
River & Rowing Museum (Henley)
Royal Botanic Gardens (Kew)

1-3 UK Pavilion, Expo'05, Aichi, Japan
    (Mawdesley © 2005)
4-6 National Waterfront Museum Swansea, UK
    (Vile © 2005)

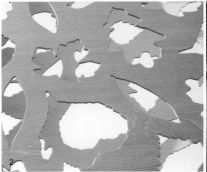

# Reinvigorate
## Total Brand Experience

2 Gads Hill / Trimmingham Road / Halifax HX2 7PX
T +44 (0)1422 340 055 / F +44 (0)1422 340 055
martin@reinvigorate.co.uk
www.reinvigorate.co.uk

**Contact** Martin Monks
**Staff** 12 plus specialist Project Managers
**Founded** 2003 **Memberships** Chartered Society of
Designers, Marketing Society

**Company Profile**
Reinvigorate deliver a total brand experience from
the creation and conception of the brand through
to the full brand experience in store. We have
the capabilities and expertise to deliver profitable
business and design solutions for any brand. Not only
do we design the brand experience we also Project
Manage the installation and construction of the full
retail environment within the client's specified budget.

**Clients**
Adams Childrenswear
Arkadia International
Boots Plc
Calderdale College
English Heritage
Fortunae Plc
Go Outdoors
Hallmark Cards Plc
H. Brown
Intimas Group Plc
Marks & Spencer Plc
Pearsons Group
Things International

**See also Branding and Graphic Design p. 80**

# Sheridan & Co
## Creating the Difference

Riverside / Market Harborough /
Leicester LE16 7PT / Leicestershire / UK
T +44 (0)1858 468 000 / F +44 (0)1858 463 444
enquiry@sheridanandco.com
www.sheridanandco.com

56A Poland Street / London W1F 7NN / UK
T +44 (0)20 7292 3333
enquiry@sheridanandco.com
www.sheridanandco.com

111 Wooster Street #4A / New York NY10012 / USA
T +1 (0)212 625 1666 / F +1 (0)212 625 1412
enquiry@sheridanandco.com
www.sheridanandco.com

**Management** Michael Sheridan
**Contacts** Marcus Flounders – General Manager UK,
John Dupuis – General Manager USA
**Staff** 81 **Founded** 1983

### Company Profile
Sheridan & Co is an award winning Retail Design
agency. We are driven by our experience, insight and
above all commitment to creativity. We are renowned
for our innovative approach to projects that make
brands stand out from the others. With over
20 years of experience in the industry, we have gained
an enviable reputation and prestigious client list,
achieved through delivering a consistent standard of
overall service, based on in-depth market knowledge,
speed, responsiveness, attention to detail and a culture
devoted to innovation. We are the experts in bringing
your brand vision to life.

With offices in the UK and the US we are easily able
to meet global demands with consistent execution.
We provide a full range of services; from creative
design, manufacture, print production, multimedia
design to shop installation. These facilities, coupled
with experience and insight, result in outstanding
retail site installations, promotional launches and
point of purchase units for luxury goods in prestige,
specialist, domestic and travel retail stores.

Sheridan & Co is committed to understanding your
brand vision and delivering it with competence,
innovation and passion.

### Clients
Procter & Gamble
Clarins
William Grant & Sons
L'Oreal
Estee Lauder
Elemis
Laura Mercier
Selfridges
Nars

1 Lab Series Retail Site, with interactive tester bar,
  Brown Thomas, Dublin
2 Elemis Retail Site, Harvey Nichols, Knightsbridge
3 Elemis Retail Site, Spa Pod Interior, Harvey
  Nichols, Knightsbridge

# Start Creative Ltd

Medius House / 2 Sheraton Street / Soho /
London W1F 8BH
T +44 (0)20 7269 0101 / F +44 (0)20 7269 0102
jen@startcreative.co.uk
www.startcreative.co.uk

**Management** Mike Curtis and Darren Whittingham
**Contact** Jen McAleer
**Staff** 66 **Founded** 1996 **Memberships** D&AD, DMA,
DBA, IVCA

### Company Profile
Great ideas are rare, yet it is ideas that differentiate
organisations and create value. The best ideas are
also borne of collaborative thinking and working
together.

For over a decade, pursuing this way of working has
allowed us to build lasting relationships, to surprise
and delight our clients and to connect them to their
audiences.

### Clients
Virgin
BBC
Royal Mail
Hertz
uSwitch
Transport for London
Department of Health
COI Communications
Bentley Motors
Up My Street
Visit Britain
Air Partner
Fox Williams
Azzurri

### See also Branding and Graphic Design p. 86
and New Media Design p. 148

1  Virgin Mobile Underground store
2  Virgin Mobile catalogue
3  Virgin Mobile Bites magazine
4  Virgin Mobile phone packaging

1

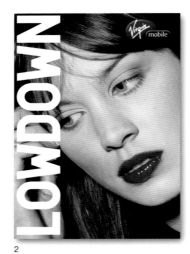

2

3

4

# Tibbatts Associates Ltd
## Design Consultants & Architects

1 St Pauls Square / Birmingham B3 1QU /
West Midlands
T +44 (0)121 236 9000
info@tibbatts.co.uk
www.tibbatts.com

**Contacts** Carmel Watts, Adrian Abel
**Founded** 1979

### Company Profile
Tibbatts Associates' team was established in 1979 and has for the past 30 years specialised in the Leisure, Hospitality, Hotel and Entertainment industry.

The firm's track record is long established, with considerable breadth of activity in projects ranging from the one-off small independent restaurant to the £100M+ holiday village development, covering hotel, bar, cinema, theatre, casino, F&B, fine dining, health & fitness, spa and all stops between.

Whilst the bulk of Tibbatts' work is in the UK, the firm has designed venues in the Far and Middle East, Europe, Africa and North America, collaborating with consultants, clients, suppliers and contractors worldwide.

Tibbatts' professional team comprises a blend of designers, architects and technicians with project planning and management support, ensuring that projects are creatively conceived and technically executed to a proper time and cost discipline.

The longevity of Tibbatts' success has been in the close collaboration between achieving client objectives and the production of commercial, quality, design solutions.

For the latest information please email info@tibbatts.co.uk. Or checkout our website: www.tibbatts.co.uk.

# Two by Two
## Design Consultants

348 Goswell Road / London EC1V 7LQ
T +44 (0)20 7278 1122 / F +44 (0)20 7278 1155
zebra@twobytwo.co.uk
www.twobytwo.co.uk

**Management** Salvatore Cicero, Ashwin Shaw
**Contact** Nikki Wollheim
**Staff** 7 **Founded** 1995 **Membership** BDA

### Company Profile
Small is beautiful and particularly so in our world.
There are 7 valued team members at Two by Two,
working to an ethos and in an environment that
encourages creativity, resourcefulness and self
development.

Both partners are actively involved in the planning,
management and art direction of all projects. We
offer a dedicated team and personal service for each
client, combining a blend of fresh creative ideas,
with extensive experience of the processes involved
in translating visual ideas into practical workable
solutions.

The success of our particular approach to design
is demonstrated by the long-lasting and close
relationships that we build with our clients,
culminating in a product of which we are all proud.

Two by Two believe in the power of creativity and the
craft of implementation. And it works.

Originality breeds content.

### Clients Include
Biotherm
Cottages to Castles
Cosmedicate
Elemis
Goldman Sachs
In Harmony
Intermix
L'Oréal Group
Magnelli Coffee
Nicole Farhi
The Royal Mint
Sainsbury's
Saki Bar and Food Emporium
Teenage Cancer Trust
Triumph
Verco
The Wine Society

### See also Packaging Design p. 128

1-3 Eline Orthodontic Practice – interior design and
corporate identity, Harley Street, London
4-6 Private residence – interior design, Smithfield,
London

194

# Philip Watts Design

32b Shakespeare Street / Nottingham NG1 4FQ /
Nottinghamshire
T +44 (0)115 947 4809 / F +44 (0)115 947 5828
sales@philipwattsdesign.com
www.philipwattsdesign.com

**Management** Philip Watts **Contact** Philip Watts
**Staff** 10 **Founded** 1994

### Company Profile
Formed in 1994, Philip Watts Design has continually
grown both in size and creativity.

Our highly successful creative architectural
ironmongery range, spearheaded by the innovative
portholes for doors kits, has helped to form a family
of over 60 products regularly specified for both
national and international products by some of the
most respected architects currently working.

This design-and-build mentality has helped to
push the interior side of the business forward with
increasingly challenging projects and installations.

Our strengths rest in developing full concepts from
name generation through to the opening night; we
work closely with our clients and are flexible enough
to accept unforseen deviations and changes to
original specifications.

The Philip Watts Design style is usually signified by a
subtle blend of creativity, experience and irreverence.
This can be found in any of our projects from melting
aluminium staircases to Alsace influenced bar
concepts.

### Clients
YO! Sushi
Virgin
BBC
Channel 4
LWT
Heathrow Airport
Burger King
McDonalds
Costa Coffee
Disneyland Paris
Conran
Gillette
Seymore Powell

1-2 YO! Sushi restaurant, Brighton, YO! Sushi, 2005
3-5 YO! Sushi restaurant, My Hotel, YO! Sushi, 2006
6-7 YO! Sushi restaurant, Bluewater, YO! Sushi, 2006
8-9 Contemporary office space, Nottingham, FHP
    City Living, 2004
10 Bespoke glass bridge and helical stairs, private
    client, 2004
11 Kingly Club members bar, Soho, London,
    Richmond Developments, 2003
12 Stainless steel lozenge porthole kit, in-house
    product range, 2002
13 Cast aluminium amorphous pull handle, in-house
    product range, 2002
14 Stainless steel porthole kit with bubble viewing
    panel, in-house product range, 2003
15 Cast aluminium bar stool, in-house product
    range, 1995
16 Cast metal organic urinal, in-house product
    range, 2004 *FX Award winner
17 Sausage Bar, Nottingham, Ever 1956, 2004

7

11

17

# 3form Design

## In a world overwhelmed by choice, innovation has become the last legitimate means of securing an unfair advantage...

Unit 63 - The Innovation Centre / Caxton Close /
Andover SP10 3FG / Hampshire
T +44 (0)1264 326 306 / F +44 (0)1264 326 308
info@3formdesign.com
www.3formdesign.com

**Contacts** Austen Miller, Ben Biswell
**Staff** 6 **Founded** 2000 **Membership** BDI

### Company Profile

At 3fD we employ a gated development process where we place emphasis on the end-user to ensure that our clientís products gain the maximum possible commercial recognition. Our transparent cost structure empowers our clients to feel more in control by allowing cost commitment to grow in line with confidence.

This approach, together with our Design/R&D facilities within the UK and manufacturing facilities in the Far East, means that we offer a service that covers every element of the product development process from concept to boxed delivered item ready for market.

3form Design – Innovative Product & Packaging Development with a commercial focus.

1-3 Rugged PDA suitable for Military & Extreme Sports environments.

4 Our R&D department have developed many manufacturing techniques that offer advantage through reduced time, component numbers & cost.
Featured images are of our Non-spill rim-cups; Flashing Beacon 'Flywheel' technology and 'Wire-weld' (a technology that allows plastic to be sealed without glue, ultrasonics or screws reducing electronics damage and adding security to Europe's most widely used Chip & PIN handset).

5 Packaging: A variety of packaging solutions created by 3form Design. The designs include innovative ways of applying or dispensing the product.

6 Norwegian Design Council/Jensen Beds: The Council conducted a search across Europe and selected a short-list of agencies to promote effective design. Just two from the UK were appointed, 3fD and PDD. 3fD devised an independent spring system increasing comfort and reducing the volume of material required for the mattress.
3fD were the only British company to qualify for the final stage.

7-9 3form were asked by Bass Breweries to devise an innovative way of promoting beer at the point of sale by changing the experience of the customer. By using UV light and engineering miniature dry ice jets to chill the beer we provided all the theatre for a new marketing advantage. The design enhances every aspect of the end-user experience through improved flavour, consistent temperature control and futuristic delivery.

1

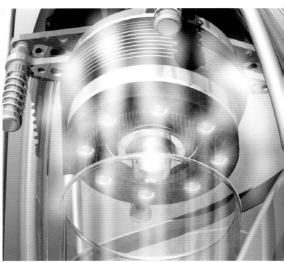

4

7

3

6

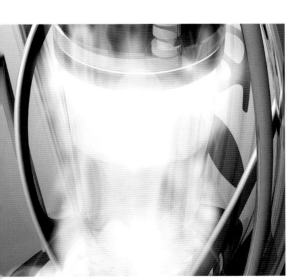

UV
protection sheild

lightstroke system

▲Bass

Lightstroke System

9

# fearsomengine

752-756 Argyle Street / Glasgow G3 8UJ
T +44 (0)141 564 3530 / F +44 (0)141 564 3500
create@fearsomengine.com
www.fearsomengine.com

**Contact** Alan Suttie
**Founded** 2002

'The fearsomengine team brings the ability to think outside the box. Ultimately they have gone the extra mile for us in delivering a quality product.'

*Mark Hoddinott, Projects and Engineering Manager DPM Water Technologies Ltd*

'fearsomengine brings top drawer design and mechanical engineering expertise to the table along with strong ideas and the ability to manage the project. We see them as part of our team – they have helped us develop a world-beating product.'

*Dr Stephen Cadden, Technical Director Rawlplug Ltd*

'The fearsomengine service was excellent. They have the expertise to turn creative ideas into products. They know what does and doesn't work.'

*John Lyons, Director Vivid Effect Ltd*

'fearsomengine's combination of strong mechanical design with expertise in aesthetics and ergonomics complemented our in-house capabilities and ensured an excellent solution to our product requirement.'

*Dr Neil Polwart, CEO Hydrosense Ltd*

# FSW Design Limited

14 Main Street / East Bridgford /
Nottingham NG13 8PA
T +44 (0)1949 21202 / F +44 (0)1949 21021
info@fswdesign.com
www.fswdesign.com

**Contacts** Philip Forrest Smith, Miles Wills
**Founded** 1995

## Design Awards
Design Week Awards 2005 – Commendation
Plastics Industry Awards 2002 – Winner

## Company Profile
Creating a commercially successful product requires creative, technical and strategic thinking.

FSW Design Limited specialise in partnering clients through a product development programme seamlessly encompassing all of these key elements.

We strive for creative answers, producing desirable products, which offer unique selling features in the marketplace.

Sound engineering practice and creative design are interdependent. A full and detailed understanding of the latest manufacturing processes and technologies ensures production issues are considered even at the earliest stages of product development. This not only produces elegant engineering solutions, but, offers our clients the financial benefits of reduced manufacturing costs.

Our product design facilities are fully integrated with FSW Multimedia, experts in providing marketing support through the use of both printed and digital media.

FSW Design Limited offer a proven design capability, increasing our client's sales and profits through the development of innovative, class leading products.

1  B&Q - Lifestyle Watering Can.
   Contemporary lifestyle product.
   Instrumental in raising the perceived quality of our customer's brand.
   Fully managed Far Eastern tooling programme.
   European marketing opportunities created.
2  Birchwood Products – Spider Ball.
   Extremely robust 4 way splitter unit for the Defender Power and Light brand.
   Designed for high durability in tough industrial applications.
   Innovative cable management facility with flexible retaining strap.
   Integral carry handle and interlocking stacking feature.
3  Skipper – Barrier.
   An innovative design solution to an everyday problem.
   Complete product development programme, including rapid prototyping.
   Full project management provided.
   Tooling sourced and fully managed.
   Awarded a commendation at the Design Week Awards 2005.
4  Fiskars – Professional Ultra Knives.
   Contemporary styling, which conveys a high quality image.
   Ergonomic improvements established through prototyping and user trials.
   Fully supported marketing programme, including the creation of an animated promotional video.
5  Siemens – Helios Signal Head.
   Innovative modular system.
   Unique anti-impact feature, providing protection against damage from a glancing blow.
   3 patents granted.
   Winner of the Plastics Industry Award, Industrial Product Design category 2002.

FSW
Design Limited

2

3

5

# Jab Design
## Clever machines
## and useful design

57 Blundell Street / Liverpool L1 0AJ
T +44 (0)151 707 7840 / F +44 (0)151 707 7841
jab@jabdesign.co.uk
www.jabdesign.co.uk

**Management** Jonathan Butters, James Bell,
Bernardo Velasco, Lee Dewson, Charlotte Corke
**Contact** Jonathan Butters
**Staff** 12 **Founded** 1999
**ISO9001:2000 – design and prototyping**

International award winning technology development
and product design consultancy, specializing in
developing innovative products.

Jab Design is structured to plug into small, medium
and large organizations to provide innovative capacity
for developing new technologies, products and
systems. We cross over between conventional
product design, product engineering and design for
cost effective manufacture (including the Far East).

We have 250 square metres of flexible product
assembly space to help bridge the gap between
prototyping and early, high value product
manufacture. A broad range of technical consultants
extend our knowledge base on a project by project
basis to include aerodynamics, optoelectronics,
instrumentation and control. Jab Design is actively
seeking project partners to jointly develop new
opportunities.

1 Garden Gopher for Benacourt International
2 MOB Guardian for RNLI Lifeboats/NTL/McMurdo
3 Cellspint for Genial Genetic Solutions
4 Caedo paper cutter for Invenio
5 Hoverwing for Hoverwing

2

4

1

3

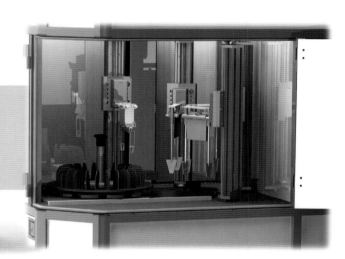

5

## Kinneir Dufort
## Design Strategy
## Innovation Brand

5 Host Street / Bristol BS1 5BU
T +44 (0)117 901 4000 / F +44 (0)117 901 4001
amy.dumas@kinneirdufort.com
www.kinneirdufort.com

**Management** Jim Orkney **Contact** Amy Dumas
**Staff** 35 **Founded** 1977 **Memberships** DBA, Institute
of Packaging

At Kinneir Dufort, we specialise in helping companies
develop their businesses by using innovation.

We are an award winning product design consultancy
with over 30 years' experience, providing successful
creative solutions across a wide range of sectors.

Inventive, responsive and reliable, our approach to
innovation is unique: our creative skills range from
concept development to mechanical engineering and
our in-house facilities include user research and rapid
prototyping. We offer an effective and comprehensive
turn-key service.

Using dynamic and adaptable tools, we generate
leading insights and consequently we know how
to make a difference. Our product development
positively affects not only our clients' return on
investment, but also makes a real impact on people's
lives.

1   ITS Netrix Trading System, BT
2   Roller Ball Mouse, Kensington
3   HandiHaler, Boehringer Ingelheim
4   Scholl Blister Plasters Pack, SSL International

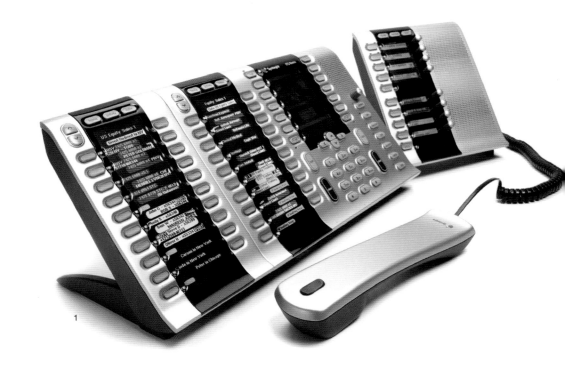

1

2

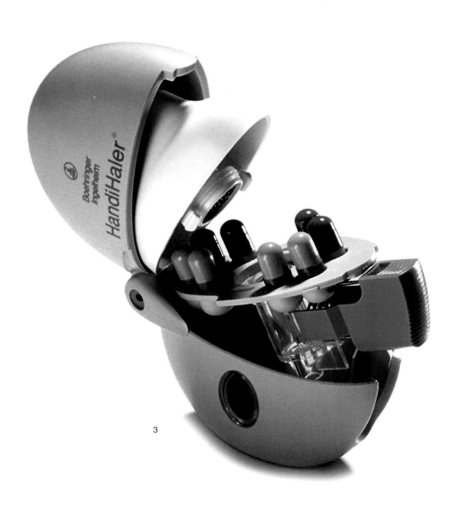

3

4

# Andrew Lang Product Design Limited
## Integrated Product Innovation

Space 1 / Fitzroy Studio / Abbot Street /
London E8 3DP
T +44 (0)20 7249 4108
andrew@andrewlang.co.uk
www.andrewlang.co.uk

**Management** Andrew Lang **Contact** Andrew Lang
**Founded** 2003 **Memberships** ACID, CSD, D&AD, RCA
**Recent Design Awards** D&AD, Design Week, Plastic
Industry, Lighting Association

ALPD specialise in integrated product innovation.
Creative insight, technical knowledge and a practical,
hands-on approach are fundamental to our design
process.

With a strong background in design for manufacture
our projects include capital and consumer product
design, furniture and lighting. Our combined creative
design and engineering skills produce intelligent
commercial solutions that work.

Our work also shapes the experience of the customer.
A positive and personal reception is important, it will
promote value and profit – the ultimate product.

**Clients**
Alfred Dunhill
Cycloc
DIY Kyoto
Established & Sons
Screen Technology

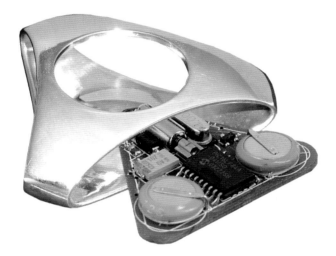

**210**

**simple solutions are best**

cycloc®

# Maddison Limited
## Product Design

Walnut Tree Yard / Lower Street /
Fittleworth RH20 1JE / West Sussex
T +44 (0)1798 865 711 / F +44 (0)1798 865 742
info@maddison.co.uk
www.maddison.co.uk

**Management** David Maddison
**Contacts** David Maddison, Sara Calder-Jones
**Staff** 7 **Founded** 1986 **Memberships** BDI, EDI

### Company Profile

Maddison is a medium size innovation and
development team with over twenty years experience
of successful design work for the medical, lifescience,
consumer and industrial markets.

From early research and brainstorming events
to detailed manufacturing specification and
product procurement, Maddison have the skills
and experience to provide the most cost effective
development plan.

Innovation is the core of our business, providing
exciting business opportunities through new
approaches and technology. We have developed
close partnerships to provide total solutions for our
clients; these include: Electronics, Antibody R&D,
Regulatory Affairs and Research.

Our client base is an exciting mix of global giants
and start-up companies, the latter often spun out of
universities and other institutions. Although our base
is in the South of England (near Gatwick), a large
percentage of our business is in the US and the
Far East.

### Clients

P&G
Reckitt Benckiser
Johnson & Johnson
Suncorp Technologies
Airflow Developments
Medical Predictions
Gulmay Medical
University of Manchester
University of Cambridge
Oxford Biosensors
Kings College London

### Awards

Star Pack – Nelsons Clikpak Pill Dispenser
Design Effectiveness – Nelsons Clikpak Pill Dispenser
Millennium Product – Nelsons Clikpak Pill Dispenser
Millennium Product – Medic-Aid HaloLite Drug
Delivery Device
BBC Design Award (Short list) – Tripod Blood
Pressure Monitor
DIY Product of the Year – Fisons 'Zap Cap' System
Ventilation Product of the Year – Greenwood
Commercial Fan
Safety Product of the Year – Pyroban System 3000
Innovation in the use of Plastics (Horner Award) –
Vent-Axia Heat Exchanger
Medical Futures 'Best Diagnostic Innovation' Award
(2003) – University of Cambridge Urine Collector
Red Dot Design Award (2005) – Airflow iCON
Ventilation Fans

reddot design award

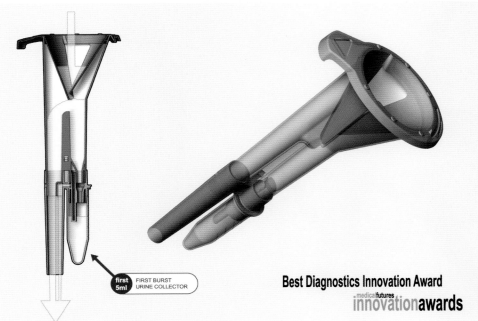

first 5ml FIRST BURST URINE COLLECTOR

Best Diagnostics Innovation Award
medical futures
innovationawards

PRODUCTS MILLENNIUM

starpack

# Tangerine Product Design

Unit 9 Blue Lion Place / 237 Long Lane /
London SE1 4PU
T +44 (0)20 7357 0966 / F +44 (0)20 7357 0784
martin@tangerine.net
www.tangerine.net

**Management** Martin Darbyshire, Don Tae Lee,
Mike Woods, Matt Round **Contact** Martin Darbyshire
**Staff** 15 **Founded** 1989 **Memberships** DBA, CSD,
RSA

### The Past
In the late 1980s, founding partners Martin Darbyshire
and Clive Grinyer identified the need for a product
design consultancy built on a new business model.
Instead of creating products based merely on
superficial aesthetics, they planned to design
products that met a genuine consumer need and
delivered a demonstrable difference. It was the belief
that product design needed to be more aligned to
a company's overall business objectives so it could
make a tangible contribution to the business.

Jonathan Ive and Peter Philips joined them and
a thriving business was established. Three of
the partners have since moved on to face new
challenges. Most notably, Jonathan Ive is now
Senior Vice President of Industrial Design at Apple
in California. Meanwhile, Martin Darbyshire continued
to grow the business, with Mike Woods, Matt Round
and Don Tae Lee joining the team.

### The Present
Tangerine is now a limited company with studios
in London and Seoul. All four key personnel are
shareholders within the business.

Over the years, tangerine has always remained true to
its founding principles. Whether conducting research,
preparing design guidelines or developing actual
products, tangerine always considers the broader
business context of a project.

1   I-River MP3 player packaging
    (in collaboration with our partner AIG)
2-3  Samsung digital cameras
4   Digit Wireless 'fastap' mobile phone

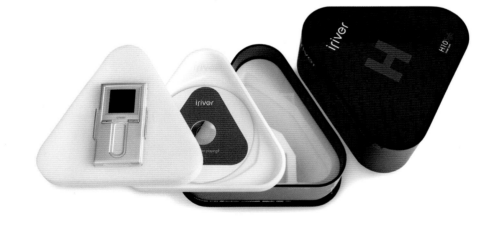

1

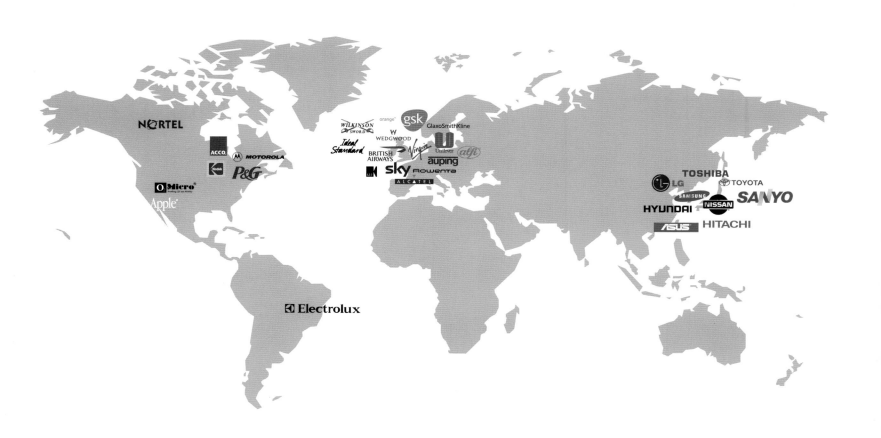

# TKO Design
## Product Design Consultants

37 Stukeley Street / Covent Garden /
London WC2B 5LT
T +44 (0)20 7404 2404 / T +44 (0)7900 681241
mail@tkodesign.co.uk
www.tkodesign.co.uk

**Management** Andy Davey MDes RCA,
Annie Gardener MA RCA
**Contact** Andy Davey or Annie Gardener
**Founded** 1990 **Membership** D&AD

### Company Profile
TKO is an independent product design consultancy
specialising in innovation. It offers a highly individual
design service which combines the highest creative
standards with commitment and enthusiasm; over
fifteen years' international experience and a genuine
desire to deliver design that represents quality and
value for money.

Since its formation in 1990, TKO has collaborated
with some of the largest global corporations, with
specialist producers and new business start-ups, as
well as advertising, marketing and branding agencies
in the UK and overseas.

The companies we work with are among the best in
their fields, and their repeat business is a testament
to how much our clients value our creativity, integrity
and commercial sense.

We are a small creative studio, light on its feet, able
to respond quickly to clients needs with freshness
and attitude, without the burden of complex
hierarchies. We create bespoke teams specifically
for larger projects, working with our own freelancers
and selected specialists, who may be bought together
to focus on specific tasks; all under the leadership of
TKO's creative director Andy Davey.

### Clients
Alcatel Telecom (France) – telecommunications
BenQ (Taiwan) – new product development
Canon Inc. (Japan) – npd, digital cameras
Daiko Electric Co. Ltd. (Japan) – commercial &
domestic lighting
De Beers (UK & US) – structural packaging
Fujitsu (Japan) – npd & consumer research
Hasbro (US & Europe) – toys & games
Honda R&D Co. Ltd. (Japan) – R&D
Kokuyo Inc. (Japan) – furniture and npd design
LEC Inc. (Japan) – housewares
LG Electronics Inc. (South Korea & Europe) – npd
NEC Corporation (Japan) – npd, computer electronics
Oxford Instruments Medical (UK & US) – medical
products for obstetrics & microanalysis
Sanyo Electric Co. Ltd. (Japan & UK) – consumer
electronics & trends research
Seiko Corporation (Japan) – eyewear
Sony Corporation (Japan) – audio-visual products
& telecommunications
Tomy (UK) – pre-school toys & baby products
Toshiba (UK) – consumer electronics
Yamaha (Japan) – musical instruments npd

1   Toshiba
2   Titan Washing Machine Ltd
3   Hasbro
4   WTC
5   Sony
6   Oxford Instruments
7   De Beers
8   Yamaha
9   Tomy
10  Yamaha
11  Tomy
12  TKO/Omega

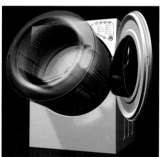

10

7

6

8

9

11

12

# Advertisements

**Bulo Office Furniture**. Showroom London: The Vanilla & Sesame Building, Butler's Wharf 43, Curlew Street London SE1 2NN - Phone 020. 7403 6993 Fax 020. 7403 5075 - info@bulo.be - www.bulo.com

**NORMAL COLLECTION - Design Jean Nouvel for Bulo**
Europackaging, Birmingham (UK) - Architects www.archemist.com - Photo www.cloud9leeds.co.uk

**BULO®**
OFFICE FURNITURE

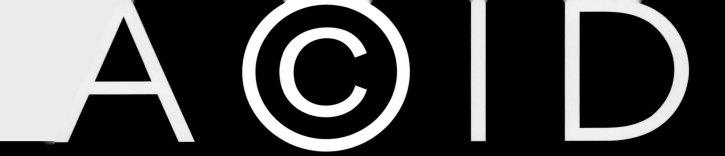
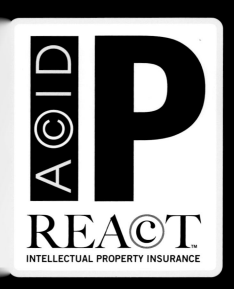

spinhex&
industrie
drukkerij

creative printers

strekkerweg 41, 1033 da amsterdam, the netherlands, www.spinhex-industrie.nl, tel. +31 (0)20 6068888

**BIS Publishers**
International publisher for creative professionals

**www.bispublishers.nl**

# Call for Entries British Design 2009/10

The next edition of this survey of leading British design agencies and studios is scheduled for publication in the autumn of 2008. It will provide the most comprehensive profile of design in this country, offering clients both in the UK and abroad an essential guide to design services in Britain.

"This is a welcome addition to my desktop. It will be very useful, very inspiring and I will use it should we find ourselves looking for a brand agency."
Kate Cowan - Head of Marketing and PR, Hay Group

"A great showcase of the best in British design and an invaluable reference."
Lance Bates - Manager Marketing Operations, Toyota (GB) PLC

"The books provide an interesting read and it is useful to see examples of various agencies' creative work covering an array of disciplines in one definitive well presented collection of books."
Steve Bulger - Marketing, JVC UK Limited

"It is an excellently put together and a most interesting set of documents. I am sure it will prove to be extremely useful."
Dave Davies – Graphic Designer, Aramak

"The books are most impressive and excellently produced."
John Graham – Managing Director, AD Creative Consultants

"The best current overview of the creative business in Britain I have seen. It shows an unparalleled and unbiased overview of UK creative excellence, and makes a wonderful resource for creative and design buyer alike."
Graham Peake – Creative Director TWO:design

## Participating agencies 2007/08 edition

35 Communications / 3form Design / Alembic Design Consultants / BDP Design / biz-R / Blackburn's Ltd / Briggs Hillier Design / Budding / Buzzword Creative
The Cake Group / CampbellRigg / Checkland Kindleysides Ltd / Clusta Ltd / ClustaSpace / Corsie Naysmith Design / Creative Edge / Dalziel & Pow / dare!
Enigma Creative Solutions Ltd / Enterprise IG / fearsomengine / Felton Communication / Fitch / Fluid / The Formation Creative Consultants Ltd
FSW Design Ltd / Hemisphere / Identica / Jab Design / JHP Design / jones knowles ritchie / Kemistry / Kinneir Dufort / Kinnersley Kent design / Kino Design

## Get your portfolio on the design buyer's desk!

A direct mailing campaign covering the UK and the Benelux offers a very persuasive pre-subscription discount. It targets approximately 20,000 design buyers and professionals in marketing, advertising and public relations.

In addition, 1,000 design buyers within a broad range of industrial, commercial and cultural sectors will receive a complimentary copy of the volume. The list of companies will be made available to the participating design agencies.

## Be part of it and don't let your name be left out!

If you are a designer or design agency located in the UK and are interested in having your showcase profile in the next edition, please contact us.

## Contact

Contact our sales manager Marijke Wervers at BIS Publishers for Information on closure dates, conditions and how to submit your work.

**Marijke Wervers can be reached at:**
email: marijke@bispublishers.nl or
Tel: +31 (0)20 524 75 68.

Branding and Graphic Design
Packaging Design
New Media Design
Interior, Retail and Event Design
Product Design

**BritishDesign 2007/08**

"This British Design publication is very useful and a good way to spot new designers and talent."
Sarah Rowen - Best Practice Manager, Atos Origin

"As a tea company with a mainstream, multiple-stocked brand we find this publication very useful. Beautiful presentation and comprehensive design company coverage make this a very desirable reference book."
Ross Thompson - Director, Punjana Tea

La Boca / Land Design Studio Ltd / Andrew Lang Product Design Ltd / Linney Design / Lisa Tse Ltd / Lloyd Northover / Maddison Ltd / NE6 Design Consultants
Osborne Pike / Parent / pi global / Pod1 / +Prism.Brand.Architects / Pure Equator / Rareform London / Reach / Redpath / Reinvigorate / SCG London
Sheridan & Co / Springetts / Start Creative Ltd / Stocks Taylor Benson Ltd / Studio Output / Tangerine Product Design / Tango Design
Tibbatts Associates Ltd / TKO Design / Two by Two / TWO:design / Über / unit9. / Un.titled / UsTwo / Vibrandt / View / Philip Watts Design / Z3 / Ziggurat Brands

# Participating Agencies by Location

## Branding and Graphic Design

**Birmingham**
032 Clusta Ltd
042 Fluid
074 +Prism.Brand.Architects
100 Z3

**Bournemouth**
070 Parent

**Chichester**
026 Buzzword Creative

**Coventry**
024 Budding

**Edinburgh**
078 Redpath

**Eton**
034 Enigma Creative Solutions Ltd

**Halifax**
080 Reinvigorate

**Hitchin**
020 Alembic Design Consultants

**Leicester**
030 Checkland Kindleysides Ltd
098 Un.titled

**London**
018 35 Communications
028 The Cake Group
036 Enterprise IG
038 Felton Communication
040 Fitch
046 The Formation Creative Consultants Ltd
050 Kemistry
054 Kino Design
056 La Boca
062 Lisa Tse Ltd
066 Lloyd Northover
072 pi global
076 Rareform London
082 SCG London
084 Springetts
086 Start Creative Ltd
092 Tango Design
094 TWO:design

**Manchester**
048 Hemisphere

**Mansfield**
058 Linney Design

**Newcastle upon Tyne**
068 NE6 Design Consultants

**Nottingham**
090 Studio Output

**Sheffield**
096 Über

**Totnes**
022 biz-R

## Packaging Design

**Bath**
114 Osborne Pike

**Bristol**
122 Reach

**Enderby**
126 Stocks Taylor Benson Ltd

**Leeds**
106 dare!

**London**
104 Blackburn's Ltd
108 Enterprise IG
110 Identica
112 jones knowles ritchie
116 pi global
124 Springetts
128 Two by Two
132 Ziggurat Brands

**Nottingham**
118 Pure Equator

**Windsor**
130 Vibrandt

## New Media Design

**Birmingham**
136 Clusta Ltd
138 ClustaSpace

**London**
142 Enterprise IG
144 Lloyd Northover
146 Pod1
148 Start Creative Ltd
152 unit9.
154 UsTwo
156 View

**Truro**
140 Creative Edge

## Interior, Retail and Event Design

**Birmingham**
192  Tibbatts Associates Ltd

**Eton**
174  Enigma Creative Solutions Ltd

**Halifax**
186  Reinvigorate

**Kew**
184  Land Design Studio Ltd

**Leicester**
168  Checkland Kindleysides Ltd
188  Sheridan & Co

**London**
160  BDP Design
164  CampbellRigg
170  Corsie Naysmith Design
172  Dalziel and Pow
176  Enterprise IG
178  Fitch
180  JHP Design
182  Kinnersley Kent design
190  Start Creative Ltd
194  Two by Two

**Lutterworth**
162  Briggs Hillier Design

**Nottingham**
196  Philip Watts Design

## Product Design

**Andover**
200  3form Design

**Bristol**
208  Kinneir Dufort

**Fittleworth**
212  Maddison Limited

**Glasgow**
202  fearsomengine

**Liverpool**
206  Jab Design

**London**
210  Andrew Lang Product Design Limited
214  Tangerine Product Design
216  TKO Design

**Nottingham**
204  FSW Design Limited

# Addresses

**35 Communications**
Clearwater Yard / 35 Inverness Street
London NW1 7HB
T +44 (0)20 7428 9960
hello@35communications.com
www.35communications.com

**3form Design**
Unit 63 - The Innovation Centre / Caxton Close
Andover SP10 3FG / Hampshire
T +44 (0)1264 326306 / F +44 (0)1264 326308
info@3formdesign.com
www.3formdesign.com

**Alembic Design Consultants**
Bancroft House / 34 Bancroft / Hitchin SG5 1LA
T +44 (0)1462 435 441
info@alembic.co.uk
www.alembic.co.uk

**BDP Design**
16 Brewhouse Yard / Clerkenwell / London EC1V 4LJ
T +44 (0)20 7812 8000 / F +44 (0)20 7812 8399
m-cook@bdp.co.uk
www.bdpdesign.co.uk

**biz-R**
35a Fore Street / Totnes / Devon TQ9 5HN
T +44 (0)1803 868 989 / F +44 (0)1803 868 888
look@biz-r.co.uk
www.biz-r.co.uk

**Blackburn's Ltd**
1a Clarkson Row / Camden Town
London NW1 7RA
T + 44 (0)20 7383 4360 / F + 44 (0)20 7383 5739
emily@blackburnsdesign.com
www.blackburnsdesign.com

**Briggs Hillier Design**
Alma House / Wibtoft / Lutterworth
Leicestershire LE17 5BE
T +44 (0)1455 221 919 / F +44 (0)1455 221 019
design@briggshillier.com
www.briggshillier.com

**Budding**
67 Poplar Road / Earlsdon / Coventry CV5 6FX
T +44 (0)24 7671 4805
info@buddingdesign.com
www.buddingdesign.com

**Buzzword Creative**
146 St Pancras / Chichester PO19 7SH
West Sussex
T +44 (0)1243 792 146 / F +44 (0)1243 787 272
adam@buzzwordcreative.co.uk
www.buzzwordcreative.co.uk

**The Cake Group**
10 Stephen Mews / London W1T 1AG
T +44 (0)20 7307 3100 / F +44 (0)20 7307 3101
andrea@cakegroup.com
www.cakegroup.com

**CampbellRigg**
8-9 Apollo Studios / Charlton Kings Road
London NW5 2SB
T +44 (0)20 7284 1515 / F +44 (0)20 7267 4112
design@campbellrigg.com
www.campbellrigg.com

**Checkland Kindleysides Ltd**
Charnwood Edge / Cossington
Leicester LE7 4UZ / Leicestershire
T +44 (0)116 2644 700 / F +44 (0)116 2644 701
info@checkind.com
www.checkind.com

**Clusta Ltd**
31-41 Bromley Street / Birmingham B9 4AN
T +44 (0)121 604 0004 / F +44 (0)121 604 3344
hello@clusta.com
www.clusta.com

**ClustaSpace**
31-41 Bromley Street / Birmingham B9 4AN
T +44 (0)121 604 0004 / F +44 (0)121 604 3344
hello@clustaspace.com
www.clustaspace.com

**Corsie Naysmith Design**
Unit 4.06 Clerkenwell Workshops
27-31 Clerkenwell Close / London EC1 0AU
T +44 (0)20 7375 0768
k.corsie@corsie-naysmith.co.uk
s.naysmith@corsie-naysmith.co.uk
www.corsienaysmith.com

**Creative Edge**
Riverside House / Heron Way / Newham
Truro TR1 2XN / Cornwall
T +44 (0)1872 260 023 / F +44 (0)1872 264 110
mail@creativeedge.co.uk
www.creativeedge.co.uk

**Dalziel and Pow**
5-8 Hardwick Street / London EC1R 4RG
T +44 (0)20 7837 7117 / F +44 (0)20 7837 7137
info@dalziel-pow.co.uk
www.dalziel-pow.co.uk

**dare!**
3 East Causeway Close / Leeds LS16 8LN
West Yorkshire
T +44 (0)113 281 7080 / F +44 (0)113 281 7088
dare.smt@virgin.net
www.dareonline.co.uk

**Enigma Creative Solutions Ltd**
119-120 High Street / Eton SL4 6AN / Berkshire
T +44 (0)1753 496 470 / F +44 (0)1753 496 482
dominic.softly@enigmaCS.com
www.enigmaCS.com

**Enterprise IG**
11-33 St John Street / London EC1M 4PJ
T +44 (0)20 7559 7000 / F +44 (0)20 7559 7001
info@enterpriseig.com
www.enterpriseig.co.uk

**fearsomengine**
752-756 Argyle Street / Glasgow G3 8UJ
T +44 (0)141 564 3530 / F +44 (0)141 564 3500
create@fearsomengine.com
www.fearsomengine.com

**Felton Communication**
2 Bleeding Heart Yard / London EC1N 8SJ
T +44 (0)20 7405 0900 / F +44 (0)20 7430 1550
design@felton.co.uk
www.feltoncom.com

**Fitch**
121-141 Westbourne terrace / London W2 6JR
T +44 (0)20 7479 0900 / F +44 (0)20 7479 0600
david.balko@fitch.com
www.fitch.com

**Fluid**
Fluid Studios / 12 Tenby Street
Birmingham B1 3AJ
T +44 (0)121 212 0121 / F +44 (0)121 212 0202
drop@fluidesign.co.uk
www.fluidesign.co.uk

**The Formation Creative Consultants Ltd**
59 Charlotte Road / London EC2A 3QW
T +44 (0)20 7739 8198 / F +44 (0)20 7729 1950
akilby@theformation-cc.co.uk
www.theformation-cc.co.uk

**FSW Design Limited**
14 Main Street / East Bridgford
Nottingham NG13 8PA
T +44 (0)1949 21202 / F +44 (0)1949 21021
info@fswdesign.com
www.fswdesign.com

**Hemisphere**
Binks Building / 30-32 Thomas Street
Northern Quarter / Manchester M4 1ER
T +44 (0)161 907 3730 / F +44 (0)161 907 3731
post@hemispheredmc.com
www.hemispheredmc.com

**Identica**
Newcombe House / 45 Notting Hill Gate
London W11 3LQ
T +44 (0)20 7569 5600 / F +44 (0)20 7569 5656
info@identica.com
www.identica.co.uk

**Jab Design**
57 Blundell Street / Liverpool L1 0AJ
T +44 (0)151 707 7840 / F +44 (0)151 707 7841
jab@jabdesign.co.uk
www.jabdesign.co.uk

**JHP Design**
Unit 2 / 6 Erskine Road / London NW3 3AJ
T +44 (0)20 7722 3932 / F +44 (0)20 7586 7048
austin.m@jhp-design.co.uk
www.jhp-design.com

**jones knowles ritchie**
128 Albert Street / London NW1 7NE / Camden
T +44 (0)20 7428 8000 / F +44 (0)20 7428 8080
info@jkr.co.uk
www.jkr.co.uk

**Kemistry**
43 Charlotte Road / London EC2A 3PD
T +44 (0)20 7729 3636 / F +44 (0)20 7749 2760
info@kemistry.co.uk
www.kemistry.co.uk

**Kinneir Dufort**
5 Host Street / Bristol BS1 5BU
T +44 (0)117 901 4000 / F +44 (0)117 901 4001
amy.dumas@kinneirdufort.com
www.kinneirdufort.com

**Kinnersley Kent design**
5 Fitzroy Square / London W1T 5HH
T +44 (0)20 7691 3131 / F +44 (0)20 7691 3141
audra@kkd.co.uk
www.kkd.co.uk

**Kino Design**
Smokehouse Yard / 44-46 St John Street
London EC1M 4DF
T +44 (0)20 7490 5850
andrew@kinodesign.com
www.kinodesign.com

**La Boca**
231 Portobello Road / London W11 1LT
T +44 (0)20 7792 9791 / F +44 (0)20 7792 9871
eatme@laboca.co.uk
www.laboca.co.uk

**Land Design Studio Ltd**
46 High Park Road / Kew TW9 4BH
T +44 (0)20 8332 6699 / F +44 (0)20 8332 6095
info@landdesignstudio.co.uk
www.landdesignstudio.co.uk

**Andrew Lang Product Design Limited**
Space 1 / Fitzroy Studio / Abbot Street
London E8 3DP
T +44 (0)20 7249 4108
andrew@andrewlang.co.uk
www.andrewlang.co.uk

**Linney Design**
Adamsway / Mansfield
Nottinghamshire NG18 4FW
T +44 (0)1623 450 470 / F +44 (0)1623 450 471
solutions@linney.com
www.linney.com

**Lisa Tse Ltd**
56 Frith Street / Soho / London W1D 3JG
T +44 (0)20 7168 9460 / F +44 (0)20 7990 9460
design@lisatse.com
www.lisatse.com

**Lloyd Northover**
2 Goodge Street / London W1T 2QA
T +44 (0)20 7420 4850 / F +44 (0)20 7420 4858
trudi.osborne@lloydnorthover.com
www.lloydnorthover.com

**Maddison Limited**
Walnut Tree Yard / Lower Street
Fittleworth RH20 1JE / West Sussex
T +44 (0)1798 865 711 / F +44 (0)1798 865 742
info@maddison.co.uk
www.maddison.co.uk

**NE6 Design Consultants**
4 St James Terrace
Newcastle upon Tyne NE1 4NE
T +44 (0)191 221 2606 / F +44 (0)191 221 2607
info@ne6design.co.uk
www.ne6design.co.uk

**Osborne Pike**
Bath Brewery / Toll Bridge Road / Bath BA1 7DE
T +44 (0)1225 851 551 / F +44 (0)1225 858 228
steve@osbornepike.co.uk
www.osbornepike.co.uk

**Parent**
Bristol & West House / Post Office Road
Bournemouth BH1 1BL
T +44 (0)1202 311 711
mail@parentdesign.co.uk
www.parentdesign.co.uk

**pi global**
1 Colville Mews / Lonsdale Road / London W11 2AR
T +44 (0)207 908 0808 / F +44 (0)207 908 0809
hello@piglobal.com
www.piglobal.com

**Pod1**
223 Westbourne Studios / 242 Acklam Road
London W10 5JJ
T +44 (0)870 246 2066 / F +44 (0)870 246 2065
contact@pod1.com
www.pod1.com

**+Prism.Brand.Architects**
The Greenhouse / 521 Gibb Street
Birmingham B9 4AA / Midlands
T +44 (0)121 224 8270 / T +44 (0)794 924 8602
ben@prismbrandarchitects.com
www.prismbrandarchitects.com

**Pure Equator**
The Old School House / The Heritage Centre
High Pavement / The Lace Market
Nottingham NG1 1HN / UK

Australian Office / Suite 7.05 6A Glen Street
Milsons Point / Sydney NSW 2061 / Australia

T +44 (0)115 947 6444 / M +44 (0)7989 322 304
F +44 (0)115 950 4948
david.rogers@pure-equator.com
www.pure-equator.com

**Rareform London**
First Floor / 148 Curtain Road / London EC2A 3AR
T +44 (0)20 7754 5962 / F +44 (0)20 7681 3150
sales@rareformlondon.com
www.rareformlondon.com

**Reach**
Hope Chapel / Battle Lane / Chew Magna
Bristol BS40 8PS
T +44 (0)1275 332 296 / F +44 (0)1275 331 399
caroline@reachdesign.co.uk
www.reachdesign.co.uk

**Redpath**
5 Gayfield Square / Edinburgh EH1 3NW
T +44 (0)131 556 9115 / F +44 (0)131 556 9116
redpath@redpath.co.uk
www.redpath.co.uk

**Reinvigorate**
2 Gads Hill / Trimmingham Road / Halifax HX2 7PX
T +44 (0)1422 340 055 / F +44 (0)1422 340 055
martin@reinvigorate.co.uk
www.reinvigorate.co.uk

**SCG London**
8 Plato Place / 72-74 St Dionis Road
London SW6 4TU
T +44 (0)20 7371 7522
susan@scglondon.uk.com
www.scglondon.co.uk

**Sheridan & Co**
Riverside / Market Harborough
Leicester LE16 7PT / Leicestershire / UK
T +44 (0)1858 468 000 / F +44 (0)1858 463 444
enquiry@sheridanandco.com
www.sheridanandco.com

56A Poland Street / London W1F 7NN / UK
T +44 (0)20 7292 3333
enquiry@sheridanandco.com
www.sheridanandco.com

111 Wooster Street #4A / New York NY10012 / USA
T +1 (0)212 625 1666 / F +1 (0)212 625 1412
enquiry@sheridanandco.com
www.sheridanandco.com

**Springetts**
13 Salisbury Place / London W1H 1FJ
T +44 (0)20 7486 7527 / F +44 (0)20 7487 3033
all@springetts.co.uk
www.springetts.co.uk

**Start Creative Ltd**
Medius House / 2 Sheraton Street / Soho
London W1F 8BH
T + 44 (0)20 7269 0101 / F +44 (0)20 7269 0102
jen@startcreative.co.uk
www.startcreative.co.uk

**Stocks Taylor Benson Ltd**
The Forge / Unit 10 Desford Road
Narborough Wood Business Park
Enderby LE19 4XT / Leicestershire
T +44 (0)116 238 7833 / F +44 (0)116 239 3407
trevor@stbdesign.co.uk
www.stbdesign.co.uk

**Studio Output**
2 Broadway / Lace Market / Nottingham NG1 1PS
T +44 (0)115 950 7116 / F +44 (0)115 950 7924
gemma@studio-output.com
www.studio-output.com

**Tangerine Product Design**
Unit 9 Blue Lion Place / 237 Long Lane
London SE1 4PU
T +44 (0)20 7357 0966 / F +44 (0)20 7357 0784
martin@tangerine.net
www.tangerine.net

**Tango Design**
Newcombe House / 45 Notting Hill Gate
London W11 3LQ
T +44 (0)20 7569 5700 / F +44 (0)20 7569 5656
info@tangodesign.com
www.tangodesign.com

**Tibbatts Associates Ltd**
1 St Pauls Square / Birmingham B3 1QU
West Midlands
T +44 (0)121 236 9000
info@tibbatts.co.uk
www.tibbatts.com

**TKO Design**
37 Stukeley Street / Covent Garden
London WC2B 5LT
T +44 (0)20 7404 2404 / T +44 (0)7900 681241
mail@tkodesign.co.uk
www.tkodesign.co.uk

**Two by Two**
348 Goswell Road / London EC1V 7LQ
T +44 (0)20 7278 1122 / F +44 (0)20 7278 1155
zebra@twobytwo.co.uk
www.twobytwo.co.uk

**TWO:design**
Studio 37 / Hampstead House
176 Finchley Road / London NW3 6BT
T +44 (0)20 8275 8594
studio@twodesign.net
www.twodesign.net

**Über**
Royds Mills / Windsor Street / Sheffield S4 7WB
T +44 (0)114 278 7100
info@uberagency.com
www.uberagency.com

**unit9.**
The Lux Building / 2-4 Hoxton Square
London N1 6NU
T +44 (0)20 7613 3330
hello@unit9.com
www.unit9.com

**Un.titled**
21 Wellington Street / Leicester LE1 6HH
T +44 (0)116 247 1111 / F +44 (0)116 247 0909
darren@un.titled.co.uk
www.un.titled.co.uk

**UsTwo**
7-10 Batemans Row / London EC2A 3HH
T +44 (0)20 7613 0433
sinx@ustwo.co.uk
www.ustwo.co.uk

**Vibrandt**
Old Brewery / Russell Street / Berkshire
Windsor SL4 1HQ
T +44 (0)1753 624 242
lovebrands@vibrandt.co.uk
www.vibrandt.co.uk

**View**
The Penthouse / Long Island House
1-4 Warple Way / London W3 0RG
T +44 (0)20 8740 9751
bguly@view.uk.com
www.view.uk.com

**Philip Watts Design**
32b Shakespeare Street / Nottingham NG1 4FQ
Nottinghamshire
T +44 (0)115 947 4809 / F +44 (0)115 947 5828
sales@philipwattsdesign.com
www.philipwattsdesign.com

**Z3**
Loft 2 / Broughton Works / 27 George Street
Birmingham B3 1QG
T +44 (0)121 233 2545 / F +44 (0)0121 233 2544
info@z3ltd.com
www.designbyz3.com

**Ziggurat Brands**
8-14 Vine Hill / Clerkenwell / London EC1R 5DX
T +44 (0)20 7969 7777 / F +44 (0)20 7969 7788
ziggurat@zigguratbrands.com
www.zigguratbrands.com

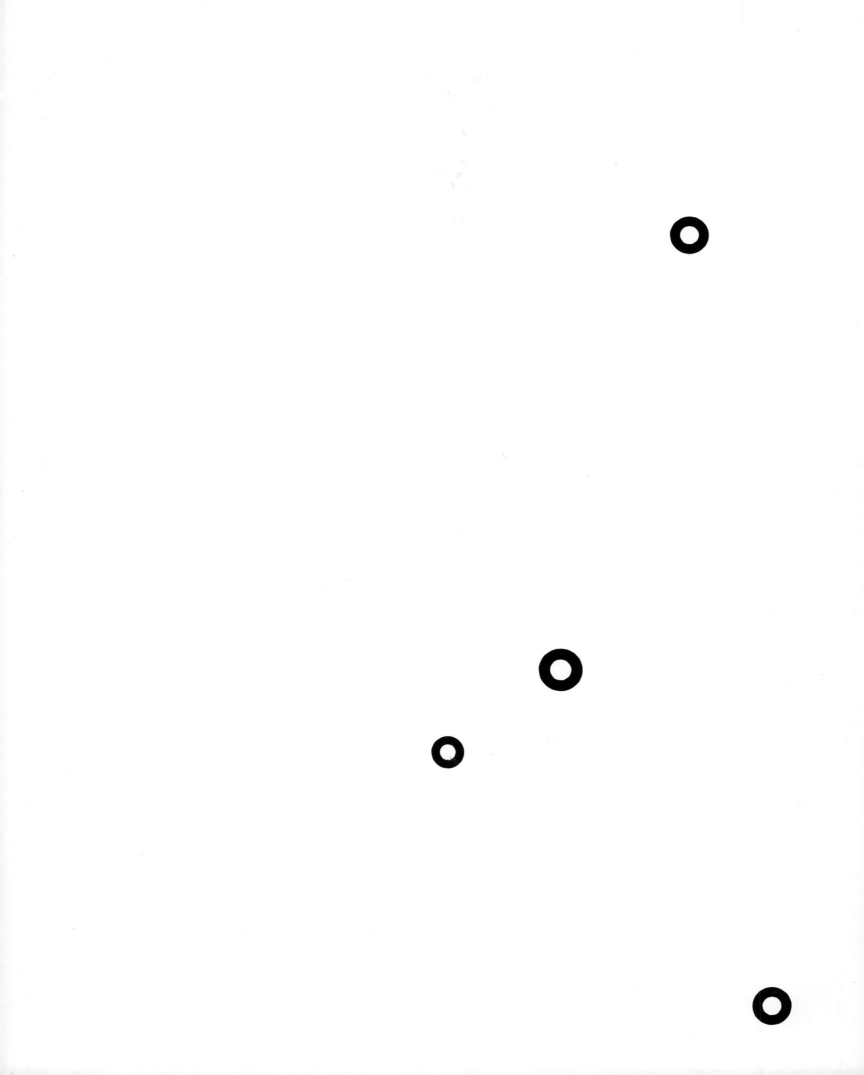

# Publication Data

**Publisher**
BIS Publishers
Herengracht 370-372
1016 CH Amsterdam
P.O. Box 323
1000 AH Amsterdam
The Netherlands
T +31 (0)20 524 7560
F +31 (0)20 524 7557
E bis@bispublishers.nl

**Sales Management**
Marijke Wervers
marijke@bispublishers.nl

**Production Coordination**
Rietje van Vreden
rietje@bispublishers.nl

**Design**
Fluid, Birmingham, UK
www.fluidesign.co.uk

**Layout**
Bite grafische vormgeving, Amsterdam

**Article**
Adrian Shaughnessy, London

**Database Publishing**
Marco Kijlstra/Iticus, Amsterdam

**Printing**
D2Print Pte Ltd